IT'S NOT A SOLO FIGHT:
SHE OVERCAME

IT'S NOT A SOLO FIGHT:
SHE OVERCAME

LASHANDRIA REDMAN
RENEE CASTILLO

Lashandria Redman

Joshua 1:9

Trilogy Christian Publishers A Wholly Owned Subsidiary of Trinity Broadcasting Network 2442 Michelle Drive Tustin, CA 92780

Trilogy Christian Publishing/ TBN and colophon are trademarks of Trinity Broadcasting Network.

For information about special discounts for bulk purchases, please contact Trilogy Christian Publishing.

Trilogy Disclaimer: The views and content expressed in this book are those of the author and may not necessarily reflect the views and doctrine of Trilogy Christian Publishing or the Trinity Broadcasting Network.

Manufactured in the United States of America

10 9 8 7 6 5 4 3 2 1

Library of Congress Cataloging-in-Publication Data is available.

B-ISBN#: 978-1-64773-316-2

E-ISBN#: 978-1-64773-317-9

FOREWORD

This book is a beautiful story about two ladies' journey with God. It is filled with encouragement, as it propels and motivates you to find your purpose and chase after God. They go on to share their pursuit in finding Him; explaining how you, too, can experience the same life-changing relationship with your creator as they did. All it takes is you making the choice to seek after Him with all your heart.

The authors explain how they found their faith in God. They teach you how they had to build their faith until they were able to take the limits off God and totally trust Him for the impossible. They do this by sharing their stories of trusting God.

LaShandria and Renee share their stories of healing. They both explain God as the creative healer that you need to trust completely, with all your heart. They go on to share the importance of trusting Him. In their stories, they emphasize how important it is to take the limits off God and trust Him with your whole heart and have faith that He knows exactly what He is doing with your life. He created you. As you trust God in this way, He perfects your faith.

This is validated through the author's personal testimonies of what God did for them. These two women were both healed through surgery instead of a sudden, supernatural experience. They share how difficult it was to trust God in this way and how they had been mocked and scoffed by other believers. Yet, they continued to trust and obey God, standing completely on His written word. They had to release their preconceived ideas of how God heals and allow Him to be the creative healer that He is. When they did this and embraced Him totally, He showed up and healed them through their surgeries.

In the end, they saw that God is the creative healer and He heals and moves in many ways in our lives. They simply go on to share their walk by faith and explain how you need to get all the limits off God and allow Him to move in and throughout your life. They explain how you must constantly read and speak His word and cancel out all fear in order to stay strong and steadfast in who you are in God. You must depend on Him daily and not allow fear to creep in and take you off track. Keep the faith and you will fulfill your purpose and become the woman of God you were called to be.

The story of their walk will both encourage and inspire every woman to be the woman they were created to be. Your faith will be made full and your eyes will be opened to truly trusting God to bring you the testimony He has purposed just for you. This book will help you build your faith and take the limits off God, so He too can become your creative miracle worker.

Dr. Michelle Corral
Foundress of Breath of the Spirit International Ministries, Inc.
Orange County, CA

PREFACE

We (LaShandria and Renee) started this journey together over two years ago. Having met and become close friends through worship dance ministry in Tucson, Arizona, we would later part ways as LaShandria moved to Oklahoma and Renee to Texas. Upon reconnecting several years later, we both discovered that we had each gone through life-threatening illnesses that had turned our worlds upside down. We believed that if God had brought each of us through our personal journeys with illness, then there was something spiritually vital that He wanted to impart to others from what we had learned. Hence, *SHE Overcame* was birthed. At the time of our trials, we did not have resources, such as this book, to guide or equip us during our personal battles. It is from this need that we felt compelled to reach out to other women and empower them with the right tools to apply the Word of God in their trials. There are many women who are silently suffering through physical illness and our hope is that this book will inspire them to stay strong and to hold on to hope in a seemingly hopeless situation. We wanted to reach out to other suffering women to remind them that God's promise of healing is evident throughout His Word, and that promise is both real and relevant to their walk-through physical trauma. This book is for all women-young, old, single, married, mothers, and wives-who have ever suffered the painful battle of an unforeseen diagnosis. This book is not just for women who are currently suffering from health battles, but also for those who will go through, or have gone through a chronic illness. We pray that these words will equip and empower you to seek the Lord and trust in His unwavering and faithful promise that because of Jesus, you too can overcome.

ACKNOWLEDGMENTS

LaShandria's Acknowledgments:

A book can be a divine way to express the heart and soul of an author. Writing a book is a journey in itself and for me, a journey that wouldn't have even occurred without the Lord and the leading of the Holy Spirit. I completely acknowledge the hand of God upon my life and upon this book, and for that I am thankful.

I am also thankful for so many other people:

First, to my husband, Covito, for the many times you would make sure I could write without distractions. I want to say thank you for your encouragement, support, always having my back, and being on the journey with me through sickness and in health.

To my children, Saniah, Micaiah, and Amaris, thank you for loving mommy and for being one of my reasons to write this book.

To my family, my mom, Sandra, my dad, Irving Sr., and my brother, Irving Jr., Aunt Jackie, Aunt Katy, Aunt Ciana, my mother-in-law, Mary, and all my family members; thank you for being there for me, praying, and loving me back to health.

Thank you to all of my friends and NDI church family for your calls, prayers, and uplifting encouragement while I was sick.

A special thank you to Erica Deguire, for the early stage feedback, editing and proofreading of chapters. Thank you for your encouragement.

Thank you to the editing, publishing, and marketing team at Trilogy Publishing. I appreciate your expertise and help to make this happen.

Thank you to Dr. Michelle Corral of the Breath of the Spirit International Ministries, for supporting our book and writing the foreword.

They say two is better than one, and I am a witness to this truth. I want to say thank you to my partner in writing, Renee. I had no idea God would bring us together to accomplish this, but I'm so glad He did. Thank you for taking the ride with me and sharing a piece of you, not only for the book, but also with me. You are my friend and my sister and I want to say thank you.

Renee's Acknowledgments:

When God first put the idea of transcribing by personal journey, I had no idea that it would one day become a published book that others would be able to read as well. God certainly has plans for our lives that far surpass the limitations of our own ways of thinking. I want to first and foremost praise and thank the good Lord for healing me and preserving my life so that I might be able to share my testimony with others. Without the comfort of strength of the Holy Spirit, my thoughts would have never made it to paper. Our God is an awesome God!

I want to thank my husband, you not only stood by me every moment of illness and recovery, but you believed in the vision of this book and supported me emotionally and spiritually every step of the way.

To my daughter, Alegra, you encouraged me even at a young age, to continue to write and share my story. Thank you for not being afraid to share Mommy's testimony with others, and thank you for being the best daughter I could ever have.

To my mother, Susan, and my father, Gordon, who always encouraged me to achieve and do my very best in school, college, and beyond. If it hadn't been for both of your support through my education and desire to write as a young girl, I would have abandoned the dream of writing a long time ago.

To Nana, who has always shown me what living a life of excellence and love should be.

To all of my family and friends who prayed unceasingly for my healing and recovery. Without your prayers, I would have lost all hope.

Thank you to Trilogy Publishing for having enough faith in SHE Overcame to partner with us and provide us this blessed opportunity.

Thank you to Dr. Michelle Corral of the Breath of the Spirit International Ministries, for supporting our book and writing the foreword.

And a deep, heartfelt thank you to my dear friend and sister in Christ, LaShandria. If you had not called me that one momentous day and asked me to take this writing journey with you, my story would have been tucked away in a journal. I am forever grateful for your vision, for your passion to serve God, and for your obedience to the Lord's call to write for His glory. God certainly made a divine connection when we joined forces, and I am so grateful to be on this journey with you. Thank you, friend.

INTRODUCTION

Life can have many blessings such as falling in love for the first time, graduating from school, acquiring a dream job, having healthy children, or even waking up each day. But life also comes with challenges and trials that we face; some expected and others unexpected. The key to navigating through life is in our response to the many blessings and trials on the journey.

What if one day, your life changed and you were challenged with a chronic illness or death? No one wants to experience the physical, emotional, and mental pain that comes with an affliction. Unfortunately, that is the current reality for so many women; and that was our reality. A reality that was presented to us as a test. Whether we passed or failed depended upon our response to the challenges we were facing.

Yet even in the trial, there is still a blessing that can be discovered. You see, how do you respond when you are challenged with an affliction or death? Is your first response to fear or rather to turn to the One that gives life and can heal every sickness and disease? "I will give you back your health and heal your wounds,' says the Lord." (Jer. 30:17 NLT)

Women are birthers by nature. We were created with wombs to carry babies and birth life. We have everything we need to care for and nourish a baby that will grow inside of us. If this is the role for us naturally, think about how this applies to us spiritually. The enemy will try to come after our "spiritual babies or seeds." If the enemy can stop us from birthing what was placed on the inside of us, that is his goal. The enemy will use anything to destroy the seed, and that includes physical, emotional, and mental affliction and pain.

If our bodies are sick and weak, we cannot fully live and walk out the purposes of God, and our seeds die because they never fully develop and are never birthed. No one who is battling a sickness or illness has the physical strength or mindset to minister the word of God to others, to pray for the brokenhearted, to feed the hungry, or to do what they were created for. Therefore, the enemy will use this attack to try to stop the message of Jesus being shared in our lives and cause us to fear, doubt, and lose hope which are all lies.

As women, we wear many hats and carry the load for our families. We are supporters of our husbands, strong for our kids, a helping hand to our friends, excellent in our careers, and surrounded by so many people each day. But somehow when faced with personal suffering, we can feel so alone in our struggle. This feeling of being alone is another lie that the enemy wants us to believe. On this journey of life, we have to learn that no matter what happens, we are not alone. The Lord is always with us. "Be strong and courageous. Do not be afraid or terrified because of them, for the LORD your God goes with you; he will never leave you nor forsake you." (Deut. 31:6 NIV)

We hear this and we know it, yet it becomes such a difficult concept to grab hold of in the midst of suffering from an illness or affliction. This is the reason for this book my sister; to serve as a testimony of how to grab a hold of the fact that God is with you before, during, and after your affliction. Whatever you will face, have faced, and are in the middle of facing right now, you don't have to do it alone. You are not alone. The Lord is with you, and there are those of us that have a testimony of walking through personal affliction and overcoming by the grace of God, and we stand with you as well.

This is our message to you; if God can heal us, then He can heal you too. Allow it to be a guide as you walk through your own personal journey. Testimonies show what God can do again and again. We hope that you are encouraged. We pray that our testimonies and what we have learned through this journey will help to release God's power in your life to bring a testimony that you too can share with others. "And they overcame *and* conquered him because of the blood of the Lamb and because of the word of their testimony, for they did not love their life and renounce their faith even when faced with death." (Rev 12:11 AMP)

"It's Not A Solo Fight: She Overcame"

TABLE OF CONTENTS

CHAPTER ONE:
THE JOURNEY BEGINS

LASHANDRIA'S JOURNEY

Let me start by introducing myself; my name is LaShandria. For over nine years, I struggled with a chronic disease called ulcerative colitis. It is an inflammatory bowel disease and autoimmune disorder that causes ulcers and inflammation in the large intestine. It changes the lining and cells of the intestine.

I would go through periods of remission where there would be no symptoms or signs of the disease, and then all of a sudden, I would get a flare-up where I would experience severe pain, cramps, discomfort, frequent trips to the bathroom, bloody stools, and fatigue. Not only did the disease damage the inside of my body, but it also affected my joints, skin and even my confidence. I felt ashamed and I couldn't understand why or how this was happening to me. No one in my family had this and I was diagnosed at the age of twenty-three.

Ulcerative colitis can be a very lonely disease especially in a world where not many people know about it or understand it. Doctors often offer textbook answers as solutions to the questions about this disease. It can be lonely because you suffer in silence from the inside out because on the outside everything can look normal and fine but on the inside, you feel so much pain; not just physically, but mentally and emotionally.

I struggled for many years up-and-down like a roller coaster ride dealing with periods of remission where I felt really great and had no symptoms and then times where the pain was extremely difficult and I didn't want to go anywhere. This disease made me feel like I was in prison, chained to the bathroom and bound by its grip on me whenever it felt like flaring up.

You see, the tricky thing about ulcerative colitis is that it affects everyone differently. There were certain foods that I could not eat because it would trigger symptoms. There were also times when I would eat a food that I thought was safe for me and it would trigger symptoms. I had to try to stay stress-free because the stress would trigger symptoms as well.

Ulcerative colitis (UC) wasn't predictable. My immune system was out of whack and my body was attacking itself and I couldn't understand why. I had gone through a lengthy period of remission right before we moved from Tucson to Oklahoma. At least it seemed to be remission; not knowing that all the time my colon was being significantly damaged and the inflammation was still there.

The move to Oklahoma was exciting yet still challenging because it was a change. When there is a change, there are going to be challenges and adjustments made. Upon arriving in Enid, my family and I faced many things that were stressors to my mind and my body. First, I was in a new place, so I didn't know anyone and we didn't have a house available to us on the Air Force base. Second, I had to go away to graduate school for three weeks and be separated from my husband and my kids. Third, I was going to graduate school and that is all I have to say. So there was a lot going on in a short period of time, and although I didn't experience direct symptoms, I am sure that my body was under some stress.

While in school, it was a challenging yet very empowering experience. In the second week of school on a Wednesday night while I was sleeping, I had a nightmare of a dream. In the dream, I was riding in the car with some people and we stopped at the stop sign. All of a sudden, a demonic figure jumped on top of the car. This figure broke and shattered the windshield, looked at me, pointed to me and said, "I'm coming for you." I believe at that moment, my like Job from the bible experience began, and my real journey with the Lord started.

I, of course, woke up from the dream a little shaken by it and began to pray. That dream occurred on Wednesday of the second week, and that Sunday going into the third week of school, I began to notice symptoms when I went to the bathroom. I started to not feel well and it seemed different than what I had ever experienced before. At first, I thought I was just getting sick with a really bad cold or maybe even the flu. I spent most of the morning in the bathroom and lying down. My classmates had brought me some medicine and other home care items to see if it would help with what we all thought was a cold.

There was a group activity planned and I was unable to go. I decided to stay in the dorm room but that meant that I would stay there all by myself. I took some over-the-counter medicine and natural remedies that I tried before and rested, but I really was not feeling well. I began to feel the cramping and aching in my abdomen and it worsened as time went on. It got to the point that I needed to get to the hospital. Everyone that I knew was gone on the trip, it was summertime so there weren't many students on campus, and it was late at night. But, I was desperate so I asked someone that I happened to find in the dorms to take me to the emergency room.

I went and I told them about my history with ulcerative colitis and they gave me some standard medicines that they give in situations like this to cover up the symptoms and try to ease the pain. The medicine they gave me worked temporarily and I went back to the dorms, but as time went on through the night and the next morning my symptoms worsened, and a day later I ended up back in the emergency room.

This time, I went to the emergency room by ambulance called on by my roommates. I was finally admitted into the hospital, especially since I had already been to the ER twice before. As I lay in the hospital bed in Colorado, fear began to overtake my mind. I was in a hospital by myself with no family close by. Although my classmates and instructors came to visit me in the hospital, I still felt alone. I know this was a plan of the enemy to make me think I was alone and to fear because the word says that He will never leave me or forsake me. After many tests and checks, I knew that I was not going to be able to leave the hospital anytime soon. I would miss my last week of graduate school and eventually end up staying in the hospital even after all my classmates had left to go home.

My I.V. had been pumped with fluids and medicine all week and I started to feel a little better. One day, before all my classmates left Colorado, I thought maybe I could catch my plane home and get back to my family, so the nurse removed the I.V. from my arm, but kept the heart monitor connected to me. I got dressed and waited for the dismissal procedures. I sat on the bed for a while and asked the nurse if I could just lie there because I was tired and started to not feel so well again. I ended up lying down and falling asleep for hours. Then all of a sudden, I remember being awakened by my nurse and many other nurses and hospital staff in the room. I was going into septic shock and I didn't know what was happening until the nurse told me. She rushed to try to get an I.V. back in me and couldn't. Then another try, and another after that, and she called other nurses to come. I eventually was stuck fourteen times before they could get the I.V. in me. I was severely sick and my body was reacting negatively. Of course I was scared, and I had a flood of negative emotions and thoughts. I thought

I was going to die and I very well could have. Septic shock is a very serious infection that can lead to organ failure. Thankfully, the nurse and other hospital staff acted quickly to prevent further damage from septic shock and I know that the Lord stopped any organ failure.

Fortunately, the hospital had my husband's phone number and called him to alert him of what was happening. He, unfortunately, could not come to Colorado, but my mom immediately flew into Colorado to be with me. After many more tests and scans, they determined that my entire colon was severely inflamed, which is called pancolitis, and I was extremely sick. I couldn't eat regular food, I was on so much medicine including steroids, I was in pain, and I was weak. I was in the hospital for two weeks in Colorado, and it would have been longer if my mom and my dad hadn't pushed for them to allow me to leave to get back to Oklahoma. I was stable enough to leave the hospital, but I was still extremely sick. I was so sick that I was escorted by a wheelchair through the airport by airport staff.

The experience in Colorado was just the beginning of this journey. Once I returned to Oklahoma, the mountain seemed to get bigger and taller. Since we had just moved to Oklahoma, I didn't have a gastroenterologist yet, and I had to schedule an appointment to be referred to see one. I only had the medicine given to me in Colorado and the pain and symptoms worsened.

After about a week and a half, I finally saw the gastro doctor and was put on a medicine that is for ulcerative colitis. I was taking this medicine and a "drug store" full of other medicines. I was on so many medications that my mom had to create a schedule for when I took certain ones. Even while on all these medications, I was not feeling better. It is an absolutely terrible feeling when your body system is full of different medications than food to nourish it. I was still in extreme pain, having frequent bathroom trips and bloody stools.

On top of that, I was not eating, I was weak, and I was losing weight. I had gotten down to ninety-nine pounds. I was too sick to take care of my kids or myself. I couldn't do normal daily functions such as bathe or dress myself. I laid in bed every day and developed muscle atrophy. I also slept most of the day partly due to one of the pain medicines that made me sleepy and because I was too weak to function. I was tired as well because I would be up at night many times in extreme pain and/or in the bathroom. I also battled against depression, negative thoughts, and to be honest there were times when I was afraid and felt so helpless.

To make things worse, I had a few trips to the emergency room in the midst of all the pain I was suffering. One particular trip to the E.R. was due to me passing out and falling in my room. I had just gotten out of the shower and I was getting dressed with the help of my husband and I stood up and I began to feel weak and sick. Then all of a sudden, I fell and thanked the Lord my husband was there because I do not remember what else happened. I was told that I had passed out and my eyes were rolling in the back of my head, my breathing was not normal, and my mom and husband called 911. The ambulance came to the house to take me to the hospital. So many attacks were coming at me physically, mentally, and emotionally. My spirit was strong because I always knew that I could turn to God, but my soul needed more strength.

One thing I know to be true is that throughout all these troubling times God was there, and he preserved my life and it taught me that I had to learn to keep my eyes on God and trust Him. I didn't have the physical strength to praise and worship but what helped me many days and nights was to listen to worship music. I would lie in the bed and just listen to the music and soak in the words of the songs. I would hear words of encouragement, the power of God, and His presence that spoke to my spirit, mind, and body. I also listened to prayers, sermons and affirmations especially at night. I found that these helped me, but they also filled my room and home with the word and presence of God. I found peace, comfort, encouragement, strength, joy, and love from doing this. It was these things along with the prayers, and love of my family that encouraged me and helped give me hope. There was a battle going on in my body and soul (mind, will, and emotions), but the atmosphere around me was full of the presence of God that it really gave me strength. In fact, I strongly believe that if I didn't have a positive atmosphere around me, I either wouldn't be here today or would have had an even worse experience.

All of this was happening as my husband still had to go to work in which sometimes, he had to be out of the state due to the military and my kids still had to go to school and be taken care of. I could not do anything but pray, cry, and sleep so my mom, my dad, my brother, and my aunts all at different times, came to help me. They not only took care of me, but also took care of my kids. They cooked, cleaned, and made sure the kids' needs were met. I would dread the nighttime, because it seemed like the pain got worse at night. Not only was the pain worse, but I felt more alone and the attack on my mind increased at night. I would sleep on and off all day, so at nighttime I would be up and my family would be asleep. I would have thoughts that I was going to die, that I would not get better, or even that I wanted to die to be relieved of the pain. This is where the healing prayers, worship music, and sermons were very helpful and effective. As I gained more strength physically, I was able to lock in and pray out loud myself. I knew how to pray before but through this I really learned how to pray and hear God. It was through these silent moments that I learned more about the intimacy that we can have with God.

One of the many significant moments I remember during this time was when my aunt came to help me. When it was time for her to leave, she decided to take my youngest daughter who was two years old at the time back to Houston with her. I wouldn't have any help because everyone had already come that could help and had to return home. I will never forget the emotions I had, a mix of sadness, worry, happiness, and peace. I was thankful that she would be willing to do that because it was so needed. There was no way that I could take care of my baby girl during the day by myself, but I was so sad as well. I was sad that it had come to that point, I felt like a failure that I couldn't take care of my child. I was sad that she wouldn't be there with us, I was scared she would miss us too much because she had never been away from us, and I knew I would miss her like crazy. However, it was the right decision to let her go and get the care she needed as I continued to fight for my health, and in the end, all was well. After my baby girl left with my aunt, I remember I cried like a baby and for the first week or two after she left I felt guilty for sending her away.

It had been a few months on the medicine I was taking for ulcerative colitis (UC), but it obviously wasn't working, and I had developed neuropathy also. So that meant I would have to add another medication to the already lengthy list I was taking. I went back to my gastro doctor and he prescribed a new medicine for UC that involved painful injections every two weeks. I had my husband give me the injections, as I could not stomach doing it myself. After a while, I started to get an allergic reaction to this medicine at the injection site, so I would take allergy medicine before.

Once I started taking this new medicine, I started to see positive changes. After a few weeks, I started to feel a little better and had fewer cramps and less pain. I started to eat, and gain weight, gain energy, and the medicine seemed to manage the symptoms. I was on a special diet eating bland foods and protein supplement drinks and I started physical therapy to regain strength in my muscles and joints and to increase endurance. I was on this medicine for a year and my symptoms didn't completely disappear, but they were managed better and the cramping pain was gone.

However, I actually started to notice different symptoms such as constipation. I went back to the doctor for a routine check and had a follow-up colonoscopy done which they found that the upper part of my colon was looking better but the lower part of it was still inflamed and I had a stricture which is a narrowing in the colon. The stricture explained why I was experiencing constipation, as well as difficult, painful, and time-consuming bowel movements. The medicine seemed to help, but it really wasn't. I continued to take the medicine as my gastro doctor told me that I should see a surgeon about having my colon removed. The presence of a stricture meant that the disease was at its worst and there wasn't much else that could be done to correct it. The stricture couldn't be reversed. I also learned that strictures usually didn't occur in ulcerative colitis and the presence of one in my case meant it could be cancer or develop into it. The area around the stricture was biopsied but they were not able to get inside the stricture to biopsy it and know for sure what it was.

All of this raised a red flag. Again, the battle raged on in my mind. Honestly, my first response was denial. I denied the fact that I was going to probably need surgery and the fact that I could have cancer. Then my next response was fear and shock. Next came turning to the Lord and that belief in the Lord helped me not to go crazy on the inside. I wish I could say that in that moment the Lord was my first response, but He wasn't. I was in a moment of pure weakness, and I, just like so many of us, respond in our human emotions. It is okay for us to have emotions because God gave us emotions to feel things like He feels things. It's okay to cry, feel sadness, be angry, and scared. But really, our first response should be the Lord. It is where we go to the Lord first and ask Him to help us and give Him our fears, sadness, pain, and anger. If we express our emotions to God under His covering, then He can help us navigate through it in a positive manner rather than how the enemy will use the emotions to destroy us. God has the capacity to help us release our negative emotions and heal from them. God will take it and turn it for good not destroy us. Just as the word says to be angry and sin not. God is saying it's okay to be angry, just don't let the anger take root to become something that destroys you or others.

As time went on I began to learn that. It is only the strength of God and faith in Him that can pull us through these moments of weakness. If we try to do it in our strength, we fail. I know it's difficult and trust me when facing life-changing news, sometimes your mind just doesn't want you to say I have to go to God. However, if and when you do, God is waiting and ready to help you.

My husband and I went to see a surgeon and then another for a second opinion. The second surgeon was friendlier, and honest yet compassionate. He told me that the way everything looked, I would definitely need to have surgery, but take time to decide when and so forth. Let's just say, it felt like a ton of bricks fell on my back. Medically everyone was saying surgery, but I had to seek God on if that was what I needed to do.

Throughout this process, I believed God could miraculously heal me, but it hadn't manifested yet the way I expected it. I lived with the stricture and the bowel movement pain associated with it for several months. During these months, we prayed, and I tried natural products like oils, supplements, foods, and any other thing I could find that may help with healing my colon or make the stricture go away. We continued to pray and believe for an instant miracle healing, but nothing changed. At that point I just wanted the stricture to go away because I did not want to have surgery. I think it was the fear of the unknown because this surgery would be life-altering. Also, who wants to go into surgery and be cut open and be exposed to all the different things that could happen and go wrong? The enemy played with my mind to make me fear the surgery. Looking back on it now, I know that the enemy was trying to get me to fear the right choice I needed to make. Time went on and I prayed and I struggled with what to do until one night I cried out to the Lord. I had done all I could do and my husband and I cried out in prayer and asked the Lord to show us what I should do. The Lord led us to have the surgery. After that, we felt at peace and moved forward with scheduling the surgery and planning for our kids.

Surgery occurred in two parts. The first part took place in March 2017. It consisted of being cut open and having my entire colon (large intestine), rectum, uterus, and fallopian tubes removed. The surgeon created a pouch with the end of my small intestine called a j pouch and connected it to my anus. The j pouch would serve as my new way of holding stool so I could use the bathroom as usual. However, this new connection would need to heal and therefore, a stoma (a small end part of the small intestine) was left out of my belly so that stool could be expelled from it. After the first surgery, it was a life-changing and a major adjustment.

Once I was released to go home, my body felt foreign. I had to now adjust to living with an ostomy bag on my belly and having stool expelled into it. It was such a struggle to deal with the ostomy bag attaching properly to my belly, having stool leaks, dealing with irritated skin, managing the pain, and healing from the actual surgery. Fortunately, I had support with a home health nurse that would come and help with the ostomy bag issues I had and to check on my recovery as well as my mom and husband.

After this surgery, I finally had some relief from the ulcerative colitis pain that I had experienced for so long, but I experienced frustration and self-consciousness about the ostomy bag. I rarely left the house and if I did, I would just stay in the car or go to appointments. During this time, my maternal grandmother passed away from cancer and I traveled out of town for the funeral with my ostomy bag and it was the most uncomfortable feeling to have to face the world wearing a "bag" on my belly. Although, I knew no one knew I had it unless I told them, I still was self-conscious and I didn't want to have any issues with the bag. But the feelings I had were so small compared to the pain my family and I were experiencing with the loss of my grandmother. My heart couldn't take any more pain, I felt like I had my share of it with everything that I had just been through, but I was so thankful that I was stronger and healthier to be able to travel for the funeral. Even with this loss, I knew that she was with the Lord and I could see how the Lord would use pain for good to keep my heart turned toward Him. I wore the colostomy bag for two and a half months as I waited for the second part of the surgery.

The second part occurred at the end of May 2017. I honestly was so ready for this part because I was tired of the colostomy bag and all the steps that went with it. I was thankful that I was feeling a whole lot better than I did before the surgery, but I was ready to complete all the steps. The second part of the surgery wasn't supposed to be as challenging as the first part. The second surgery consisted of putting the stoma back in place. After it was completed, I had to stay in the hospital until I had a bowel movement to make sure that the created j pouch was working properly. It took close to a week after the surgery for my first bowel movement to occur. I could eat regular foods with very strict restrictions and consideration.

I finally was released to go home and at home, I had a little after surgery pain, but I was feeling good. I had a hole in my belly from where the stoma was that would over time close and heal. At first, going to the bathroom was a little scary because it didn't feel the same as before surgery. My bottom would get irritated and sore easily. I would have to go to the bathroom at least 12 times per day.

After a week at home, I ended up in the emergency room. I had extreme pain in my abdomen and it was discovered that my intestine stopped working. I had to get a tube put down my nose and throat that I eventually kept in for five days. I was transported back to the hospital in Norman, Oklahoma where I had surgery. I was back in the hospital due to complications. I stayed in the hospital with a tube down my nose and throat, couldn't eat or drink anything, and had to wait until my system started working again.

Once I finally got through this setback, I was able to go home and start the transition of recovery and learning to live with a j pouch. Through it all I can truly say that God's hand was on me and His presence was with me. I didn't always realize it and I honestly didn't always feel that it was, but it was Him and only him that allowed me to live and be healed. This journey has not been easy, but I have gained so much from it. It is the Lord that gives life, because He is life.

"With long life I will satisfy him and show him my salvation." (Ps. 91:16 NLT)

RENEE'S JOURNEY

"For God has not given us a spirit of fear, but of power, love, and a sound mind." (1 Tim 1:7 NKJV)

My name is Renee and I will always vividly remember the night I took on Goliath. Fear had already crept in the back door of my mind and made a home, the kind of fear that leaves you sick to your gut, and your mind a worrisome mess. Once this kind of fear attacks, it takes you on a downward spiral to hopelessness, even despair, not being able to see what is lurking in front of you. Many will say fear is the absence of faith, and it is. Fear is a crippling affliction of the mind; the unknown is scary, but with God's perfect love, we can hold onto the faith that fear can and will be cast out. *"There is no fear in love; but perfect love casts out fear, because fear involves torment. But he who fears has not been made perfect in love." (1 Jn 4:18 NKJV)*

Already sensing something was preparing to drastically attack my body, I had tried with all my might to fight the fear by myself. God had given me a dream the previous month that I had mistakenly discerned as an oppression. In the dream, God showed me exactly what I would be diagnosed with, but I was too shocked and frightened to believe it. Despite my disobedience to God's warning, I did end up driving to the Rio Grande valley three hours south of San Antonio, where we live, to get the long-awaited -or should I say dreaded- MRI. I tried to act like I was not afraid, and to give myself a minute amount of credit, I was not that afraid, at the time. After all, God would never allow an obscure affliction to attack my health. That just could not happen to me, let alone my family. It just didn't seem possible.

We arrived at the radiologist's office only to discover their machine was down. Almost relieved, we began to make our plans to head back up to San Antonio. After relaying to the owner of the office my symptoms, he was certain I had suffered a minor stroke. The Holy Spirit told me this was wrong, but I listened as he recounted his sister's battle with stroke at a young age, and how I could not let my symptoms proceed any further without figuring out what the culprit was. As we thanked the radiologist for his time and made plans to return the next week when the machine would hopefully be functioning, he came flying into the office. "It's working, quick, let's go

Renee. You're first. I don't know what happened, but this machine was not working and all of a sudden you guys show up."

My husband and I smiled at each other, as we knew it must be God's hand. As thankful as I was, fear began to sink in again. I was running from what I knew was already there. Our heavenly Father says "Do not fear" 365 times in His Word- one for every day of the year- yet I still could not trust Him at that moment, with all my heart. *Trust in the Lord with all your heart. Lean not on your own understanding. In all of your ways acknowledge Him, and He shall direct your paths." (Prov 3:5-6 NKJV)*

I was rushed into the MRI room by the radiologist, who hurriedly gave me instructions on how to stay still, try to swallow in-between sounds, press the button if you get claustrophobic, etc. To my pleasant surprise, I found it a blessing to be able to lie there for 45 minutes and pray. I praised God over and over for "parting the Red Sea" and causing that machine to miraculously work. As we finished and the radiologist came back into the room to escort me out, I will never forget the look on his face. He tried his best to act like he didn't see anything, like all was well. But the shocked expression on his face told me something different: "If you only knew, you poor thing."

We left with a CD in hand of the results, and the assurance that they would send my results that afternoon to the neuropathic office. I felt a shallow sense of relief as we went to find a spot for lunch, do a little shopping, and play a few games of skeeball with our then 4-year-old daughter, Alegra, before heading back up to San Antonio. It was then, as I was hurling that ball up the ramp, that my phone began to ring, and ring, and ring.

Radiologist: "Hi Renee, I need your doctor's phone number right away."

Me: "He's out of town for the holiday weekend, you won't reach him."

Radiologist: "I still need it, please."

Me: "Is something wrong."

Radiologist: "If there is, he will call you back tonight."

Silence. Heart dropping, fear gripping, mind whirling. Can somebody please wake me up? We scurried out of Peter Piper, my husband and I both sensing that something big was coming, like when you see a storm in the near distance, and you know that it will hit within minutes, maybe hours, yet you cannot avoid the calamity that will ensue. I wish I could tell you that at that point I remembered sermons past, that Jesus was in the eye of the storm, holding me, cradling me in His arms, rocking me, pacifying me, stilling a sea of emotions stirring within me. Yet regardless of my own forgetfulness, my heavenly Father had not forgotten me. He was holding me for dear life that day as we jumped in the car, and as my husband began to pray over me. My husband is a full-time minister and evangelist. He has been actively working in the ministry of the gospel for over twenty years. I joined him in this ministry when we got married in 2012. Though I am a teacher by profession, my daughter and I traveled with my husband as he preached the gospel whenever we could. My husband is a man of faith, but that day when I heard the alarm in his voice, I became numb.

We never heard from my doctor that day, which meant it must not have been that serious. After all, it was a three-day weekend. Surely, he would contact me if the results showed some life-threatening conclusion? I fell asleep on the drive home listening to healing scriptures on YouTube, and singing to myself an old hymn from my childhood:

Do not fear

My little flock

for the Father is glad

to give you the Kingdom

wherever your treasure is

there also your heart will be

and the Father is glad

to be your shield.

I prayed with all my might that night in our prayer closet at home. I cried before the Lord, I danced before Him, I begged Him. "If this cup should pass..." But Jesus was not permitted to escape suffering, so why should I ask such a bold prayer? And what was my cup of suffering, I still didn't know. It was still a mysterious, unknown obstruction.

The revealing of the giant, Goliath, finally came a day after my MRI. I awoke at 2:30 in the morning to my left arm going numb, then my left leg, followed soon after by my right. I felt like 10,000 volts of electricity were being executed throughout those three limbs. I sat up long enough to vomit, and then realized that I could not walk. I screamed for my husband who came running into the bedroom from the prayer closet where he was praying, and immediately called 911. My mind was completely intact as I prayed that the Lord would preserve my mind, my brain, of all things to save. I began to praise him out loud with all of the strength I could exude through my vocal cords.

"I love you Jesus! I praise you Jesus! I trust you Jesus. God you are so good"

The Holy Spirit is still a divine mystery to me. Yet in that moment, I knew it was not me who was praying those prayers, but a true manifestation of the Holy Spirit through praise. *"My flesh and my heart fail; But God is the strength of my heart and my portion forever." (Ps. 73:26 NKJV)*

After rushing to the closest ER, we finally received the results I had been waiting for. The ER doctor was more than willing to read my MRI results from the day before and give a firm diagnosis.

"Ma'am, the good news is, we can rule out MS and all other muscular degenerative diseases by looking at your MRI results. Now, I hate to be the one to have to tell you, but you do have a large *benign* brain tumor on the left side of your inner ear and brain stem, and this can be removed by a neurosurgeon."

My husband and I began crying tears of joy! Yes, joy! Joy mixed with relief to find out that it was benign. I will never be able to understand how I could have such joy upon hearing such findings, yet I initially felt gratitude. I think part of that thankfulness was also relief that the affliction had finally been sighted, and named. Once you know the culprit, it's much easier to conquer it. Rolando held my hand tightly as we continued to listen to the doctor's diagnosis and recommendations for seeking extraction of the tumor.

Our dear pastors and friends, Jose and Natalia, came unexpectedly to the hospital while they proceeded to run an additional cat scan to confirm the diagnosis. As they rolled me back into my hospital room, I couldn't fight back the tears that engulfed my face when I saw these two dear friends waiting for me. We prayed together and I could feel their words of encouragement speak to me as if Jesus himself was standing there comforting me.

Pastor Jose spoke to me about David and Goliath and that

he was already planning on preaching this sermon that very morning, on facing our fears with the Lord fighting the battle. He spoke of how the Israelites could not stand against Goliath because of all of the other voices of the world telling them that God would not come through: our own voices inside of our heads, the voices of people in our life who may say that God cannot heal, and the voice of the enemy who tells us we have everything to fear. David heard the Lord's voice over all of the others because he focused on Him, and as a result, the Lord fought and won the battle over the giant enemy.

The voice of the Lord is over the waters;

The God of glory thunders;

The Lord is over many waters.

The voice of the Lord is powerful;

The voice of the Lord is full of majesty.

The voice of the Lord breaks the cedars,

Yes, the Lord splinters the cedars of Lebanon.

He makes them also skip like a calf,

Lebanon and Sirion like a young wild ox.

The voice of the Lord divides the flames of fire.

The voice of the Lord shakes the wilderness;

The Lord shakes the Wilderness of Kadesh

Ps. 29: 3-8 NKJV

He reminded me I would overcome by the grace of Christ if I would choose to hear the voice of GOD above all others. The voice that says, "I am healed by His stripes." The voice that says "overwhelming victory is mine in Christ Jesus." The voice that says, "do not fear, for I am with you." The voice that says, "death itself will never separate us." The voice that says, "I have called you with an everlasting love, and you are mine." The only voice that mattered in my life at that moment had to be HIS voice. Oh, that beautiful voice!

I smiled, and even chuckled as Pastor Jose shared this word with me. Only 7 hours earlier had I been watching Veggie Tales with Alegra before we went to sleep. The episode: *David Fights the Big Pickle.*

Little did I know how big the battle of brain surgery would really be. I was scheduled for a craniotomy two weeks later in Georgia by a neurosurgeon, also a believer in Christ, who came highly recommended by a friend of my father. He assured me that removal was completely possible, and that I would be "just fine." These were comforting words that I needed to hear. An expert brain surgeon did not seem intimidated by the golf ball size tumor that had grown in my head, so why should I?

My surgery was ten hours, and I think my husband suffered the most during that time. In a craniotomy, the skull is cut open so that the brain can be accessed. A computer system that is attached by "prods" that are placed throughout your head (very sci-fi looking) helped the surgeon navigate the brain. There are many risks involved in a craniotomy, the most common being stroke, but I have the Lord to thank that I not only came out alive, but I even returned to teaching dance 8 weeks later.

Although the surgeon was not able to remove the entire tumor due to the danger of severing crucial nerves in my brain (a little alarming to hear at the time, as these types of brain tumors do grow) he recommended I have gamma knife radiation surgery 6 months later to deaden the tumor cells that were left, which was about a sixth of the size of the original tumor. Of course, I agreed to this, and thus had the GK surgery when the time came.

The 11-month post-MRI indicated that the remaining piece of acoustic neuroma (brain tumor) was stable, which means that it has not grown, and it has not shrunk. For this, I am grateful.

What many people do not understand, and to this day many of my family and friends do not even know, are the multiple side effects that result from a brain tumor and partial removal of one. Even I assumed that once the brain tumor was removed, I would feel "normal" again. But, with God's help and strength, I am learning to embrace a "new normal." I am not complaining, but rather sharing my resulting symptoms and side effects in hope that you will be comforted knowing that you are not alone in your survival of the "aftermath" of illness and major surgery. Though we try not to focus on them, to completely disregard their existence might be of detriment to overall emotional and physical healing.

An acoustic neuroma grows on the nerves that run through the brain. It specifically begins growing on the nerve that controls the sense of hearing. Before surgery, I had already lost a large percentage of my hearing on the left ear, and now I have about 90 percent loss. Being deaf in one ear is certainly an adjustment, but I am always thankful that I can hear well in my right ear. I have grown to enjoy laughing with people when I can't find my phone (because I can no longer tell where sound comes from). On the plus side, I sleep very well when there is noise. My left eye no longer produces tears and becomes painfully dry on some days. This type of tumor also affects the vestibular nerve, which is the nerve that helps you balance. I have some difficulty walking straight, in open spaces, and I especially struggle at night, or in smaller spaces like halls. However, despite the balance change, I am still able to regularly teach ballet and prophetic dance, with a few trips here and there. There are also side effects from the radiation treatment that still affect me almost 18 months out. I had swelling in my brain a few months after the gamma knife and was put on steroids, as this is very risky. Some days I wake up feeling like my brain is going to push through my skull, or like I'm living in a "fog." I have two screws holding my skull back together, and a large dent in the side of my skull, which shifts frequently.

Yet despite the aftermath, I am grateful for my experience and believing in my God, who is able to completely heal me. Although there is still a small residual tumor left, I am choosing to trust that God will stop this piece from growing back, just as he stopped the storm for the disciples. I am learning that trusting Him through the unknown is a great challenge, but amidst that struggle, there is unprecedented growth and blessing.

CHAPTER TWO:
TAKING AUTHORITY

We all have different afflictions that we have experienced and even if your affliction is the same, your journey is not. Our experiences may be unique, but there is common ground among all of us that cannot be denied. When facing a physical affliction, we all know that it's not just physical pain but mental and emotional pain as well. At our lowest point of weakness and vulnerability, the enemy uses it as an opportunity to torment us, play with our emotions, and even expose insecurities we have.

There is a struggle in the mind that we all experience, and if we don't learn how to overcome the struggle, it has the power to break us down and hinder our physical healing. It is with the mind that we can bring glory to God by focusing on Him as our solution and not the problem, which means we have to take control and authority over our thoughts. *"Set your mind and keep focused habitually on the things above [the heavenly things], not on things that are on the earth [which have only temporal value]." (Col 3:2 AMP)*

Not only do we have to take authority over thoughts and emotions, but over what we speak as well. Affliction is not just a physical and natural war, but it is a spiritual war. We literally enter into spiritual warfare fighting for our lives and our mind, will, and emotions. We must recognize that we have authority and weapons that we can use to fight against the enemy and the afflictions we face. Once we really grab a hold of the promises of God and the weapon of His word, then we can stop affliction in its track and repel the enemy.

RENEE'S EXPERIENCE

We Have A Weapon in the Word

"For the word of God is living and powerful, and sharper than any two-edged sword, piercing even to the division of soul and spirit, and of joints and marrow, and is a discerner of the thoughts and intents of the heart." (Heb 4:12 NKJV)

We have all prayed for the healing of a loved one. This prayer is inevitable in the life of a believer, and even those who do not believe in Christ have undoubtedly asked an unknown God for a miracle. Yet, many times it is easier to believe in healing for others than it is for ourselves. It is easy to pray for another person's healing, but when it comes to our own, we freeze up and stumble over our petitions, falling into the belief that Jesus can't or doesn't want to heal us. It is often for two reasons that we fail in praying over our own healing. First of all, we allow shame and pride to enter into our mindset, thus giving into the lies and foils of the enemy. When we automatically believe that we are sick because we "deserve" it or have done something to bring upon us judgment through affliction, we are giving into false beliefs and hypocrisy of a religious mindset. If this were true, then the gospel message would be false, a story told in error. But as believers in the divine Word, we know this is flagrantly false doctrine. After all, Jesus died on the cross to redeem us, and through this redemption, our sins have been washed away in His blood. *"Come now, and let us reason together," Says the Lord, "Though your sins are like scarlet, They shall be as white as snow; Though they are red like crimson, They shall be as wool." (Is. 1:18 NKJV)*

Thus, when we call on the name of the Lord for salvation, we are made new, and our sins can no longer hold us in bondage. God does not "judge" us through cancer, sickness, and other life-threatening diseases, because Jesus has already sat on the seat of guilt on our behalf, to remove the charges against us. I recently read an account of God's judgment on the rebellious people of Ashdod in 1 Samuel 5. God had judged the unbelieving, idolatrous people of Ashdod by sending plagues of tumors. Now reading this a year and a half out from my own diagnosis, I froze, both perplexed and terrified, thinking for a brief moment that God had also "plagued" me with a large brain tumor because of my sinfulness. I spent an entire day seeking the Lord, reading His word, and questioning if my own sickness had been self wrought. Then I came upon the above scripture in Isaiah. God showed me in prayer that he had already paid the price through Jesus, and by accusing myself of transgression and judgment, I was actually denying the validity and power of the cross. Ouch! I quickly reconciled to God and asked for His forgiveness for doubting who He is, and what he had accomplished through His Son.

The difference in the rebellious people of Ashdod is that Jesus had not yet made the ultimate sacrifice for their sin; they were living separated from the grace and forgiveness of the most high God. Their relationship with the Almighty was severed by their worship of a false idol, and there was no one to stand in the gap. Because of this rebellion, judgment ensued through the attack of tumors. But now, we as Christ followers live under the new covenant and the Bible clearly states that *"Surely he took up our pain and bore our suffering, yet we considered him punished by God, stricken by him, and afflicted. But he was pierced for our transgressions, he was crushed for our iniquities; the punishment that brought us peace was on him, and by his wounds we are healed." (Is. 53:4-5 NIV)* So this means that every affliction was already paid for on the cross. We don't deserve affliction and it doesn't belong to us; healing does because it was bought through Christ's sacrifice.

Secondly, we fail to pray prayers of boldness for our own healing because of doubt and unbelief. We build up a false impression in our hearts of who God really is, thinking that he is too busy, or too consumed with other more important works of healing, to remember or consider us. But, this is a blatant lie from the enemy himself. God is always capable of healing, and it is His will for us to be healed. But Jesus looked at them and said, "With men *it is* impossible, but not with God; for with God all things are possible." (Mk. 10:27 NKJV)

Our own healing is completely possible because of the fulfillment of the Messianic promise on the cross. So how do we combat those evil thoughts that lurk within our thoughts, tempting us to think that God can heal anyone else, but it is not His will to heal me?

There are two approaches to fighting in the battle zone going on in the mind of a sick believer that I learned to adopt when I was in my own war of unbelief and hopelessness. First of all, we must turn to the scripture; His word becomes "the sword of the Spirit" (Eph. 6:17) in our hearts. After I received my diagnosis, I had a hard time praying. I often felt my prayers were repetitive, weak, and selfish. "Lord, please heal me. God, please make this tumor disappear. I don't want to go through this brain surgery, God." Now, there is nothing biblically wrong in praying these types of prayers. After all, the Lord promises we will get what we ask for in prayer when we trust Him.

"And whatever things you ask in prayer, believing, you will receive." (Mt. 21:22 NKJV)

Yet, the power did not come in praying with my own words, but in crying out to Him with His very own Words. When it comes to praying during the illness, it is the initial reaction to pray "Lord heal me," or "Take this away." I found later that prayers like this don't provoke the Lord to move. He won't respond to a prayer that has already been answered. He has already healed us through His blood. So it is key to pray His word and to pray what He can respond to that hasn't been done already. It is not that He doesn't understand the pain or what you are asking, it's just that the prayer of "God heal me" is like saying please make the trees green and He is saying I already have, but you have to see it, believe it, and receive it.

Every time I was alone and vulnerable to thoughts of unbelief and misery, I would play a compilation of healing scriptures I found on the Internet. I listened to these scriptures so often that they would resound in my mind, even when I wasn't intentionally praying. I would memorize them, recite them, and decree them. When we are most vulnerable in life is when God's Word is the most powerful "For when I am weak, then I am strong." (2 Cor. 12:10 NIV)

It also took a great weight off of my conscience, as I realized that I wasn't praying to God with selfish motives or petty requests. Instead, I was declaring what he had already spoken over the sickness, professing that I believed He would come through in a mighty and miraculous way. My motto would become "declare" rather than "beg." If you are battling an illness, declare the scriptures over your life and witness the peace of God, Shalom, take captive your mind and quiet your heart.

LASHANDRIA'S EXPERIENCE

We Eat of the Word for A Strong Spirit

I had been diagnosed with this disease for a very long time already before it came to the point of surgery. I had struggled physically, mentally, emotionally, and even spiritually with why this was happening to me. Even with growing up in church, knowing that God is a healer, and wanting the disease to go away, I didn't really understand the power and authority I have as a believer. Of course I wanted to be healed, but I didn't fully understand my weapon to use against this attack of the enemy. It wasn't until I matured in the Lord and the disease progressed that I began to understand the power of the word.

"By His stripes we are healed" says the word of God." (Is. 53:5 NKJV) The enemy knows it, but do we know it? This is where healing has to be our daily bread. The Bible says in Romans 10:17 that "faith comes by hearing and by hearing the word of God." So in order to increase our faith, we have to hear the word of God, but it has to go beyond just hearing the word of God. We have to eat the word of God. Each day we should renew our minds in the word, we should pray the word, study and focus on the word, speak the word, and absorb that word just as we do natural food. The word of God is our spiritual food that in turn sustains us spiritually and also naturally.

When we eat of the word, it is what keeps us strong, healthy, and it can stand against the enemy. Eating of the word develops us into not just being hearers but doers of the word. The word is a source of strength, encouragement, protection, and guidance through times of affliction. Once the word is "eaten," then our spirit begins to grow and become stronger.

"The strong spirit of a man sustains him in bodily pain or trouble, but a weak and broken spirit who can raise up or bear?" (Prov. 18:14 AMPC)

Having a strong spirit will allow you to get through anything. Willpower and determination are good, but I believe they stem from a root of having a strong spirit. If our spirits are strong then when attacks come, we will know how to stand against them. Our minds may want to veer off into fear and doubt, but a strong spirit will pull it back into right alignment with the word of God. Having a strong spirit will help us through times when the manifestation does not happen right away or the way in which we think it should because our spirit will help keep our mind and heart focused on the truth of the word. I so wanted for my colon to be healed miraculously with an instant restoration and healing, but the healing manifestation didn't come the way in which I wanted or expected it.

Our spirits are usually what are strong and our flesh is weak, but we have to build our spirits and continue to develop it so that we will be led by the spirit and not our flesh. We are created to operate in the spirit and allow the Holy Spirit to be our guide, but we sometimes don't understand this and allow our flesh to lead. Therefore, our flesh will lead us to believe the negative report, to walk in fear, doubt, shame, and more lies.

If I had allowed my flesh to guide me, then I would have remained in a place of fear and could have exacerbated my pain and the disease by speaking the lie that I was sick and was never going to feel better, or had cancer, or could die. But as it says in the word, "whose report shall you believe?" (Is. 53:1)

We are to believe and stand on the word of God no matter what the circumstance is or what it looks like. This is often what causes us to "trip" up, focusing on what the circumstance looks like naturally instead of seeing it through spiritual eyes. Having spiritual eyes is having faith like the word says, "We walk by faith, and not by sight." (2 Cor. 5:7 NKJV)

We are to live by faith and believe and not live by what we see in our natural eyesight. Again, the Lord is telling us to believe Him, to get a revelation of who He is, and to know that His word is true. Now, I know this is much easier said than done, but as your spirit becomes stronger it empowers you to believe and the word is made flesh because you live it not just read it or speak it.

Once I came to the understanding of the power of the word, I began to speak healing scriptures over my life. Even in times when I could not physically speak, I would listen to healing scriptures and affirmations. I began to allow the word to feed my spirit and therefore my soul and body. I believe that it was the word that prevented cancer from developing in my colon. You see, it is the word that endures forever and it is given to us as our sword, our daily bread, and our guide. (1 Pet. 1:25) The word also strengthened my mind. There is such a battle that happens in the mind when you face trials like these. With every pain, symptom, or setback came a thought or even an attitude that was contrary to the word. Each day and sometimes each hour require you to renew your mind. (Rom. 12:2) Just like the word says, "If there is anything of good report, meditate on it." (Phil. 4:8) I learned when the disease was at its worst, the word was my hope, my peace, and the one thing I could cling to that was stable.

In 3 John 1:2 AMP, it says, "Beloved, I pray that in every way you may succeed and prosper and be in good health [physically], just as [I know] your soul prospers [spiritually]." We are to not only be in good health in our physical bodies, but in our mind, will, and emotions, which encompasses our soul. Physical illness greatly affects the body, but if our soul is weak or broken, that is how the enemy seeks to defeat us the most. The soul is where we think and how we feel, therefore our thoughts affect our emotions and our emotions affect our actions.

For example, when I was severely sick, I had lost so much weight and could barely walk because my strength was gone. At one moment, I remember thinking I was ugly and I was too skinny. I began to think that so much that I started to feel sad and scared for people to see me. Then, I started not wanting to go anywhere or to be around people. I would say negative comments about myself and put myself down. I found that what I was thinking, feeling, saying and the actions I was taking were making my body hurt. My mind was in a state of darkness, and it affected how I felt emotionally and physically. I had to recognize what I was thinking and feeling. I remember I said something about my weight and someone reminded me that I was walking through a severe sickness and they told me that I was beautiful because I was in the hands of the Lord. They asked me, did God think about me the way I did so negatively. It made me aware of what was happening at the time; I was allowing the enemy to destroy me, not only physically, but in my soul (mind, will, and emotions).

This is why it's so important to guard what we see and hear because they are seeds that get down in us and produce either good or bad fruit. The Lord wants us to prosper in every way, which means He wants us whole. The enemy wants to mess up our minds and cause a spiral effect of destruction in our soul, body, and therefore our lives. If our soul is weak, then it can stop our forward movement and our bodies stay weak and ultimately our lives are in turmoil and our purpose stopped. We have to take control of our thoughts and emotions before they lead us into wrong paths of darkness. But, if our spirit and soul align with God's word, then our body will be able to heal. "For the weapons of our warfare are not of the flesh but have divine power to destroy strongholds. We destroy arguments and every lofty opinion raised against the knowledge of God, and take every thought captive to obey Christ." (2 Cor. 10:4-5 ESV)

We can take every negative thought and emotion captive by the word of God.

There is power in God's word and His word brings us closer to who He is and draws us into His presence. It is in His presence that we can discover what He wants us to do and get on the same frequency with Him.

Right before I knew that God was telling me to have surgery to remove my diseased colon, I struggled with what decision I should make. I heard different opinions from people with good intentions, but I was so confused. It wasn't until I got into the presence of God through His word and prayer that I began to see my path of life clearly. I was so focused on myself, the sickness, and others, that I forgot to make sure to get into the presence of God, put Him first, and find out what He really wanted me to do. Once I began to do that consistently, then the choices I needed to make became easier. One thing I have learned is that the Lord is good no matter what, and His word is true. It is the power and presence of God through His word that we have access to, in order to help us overcome anything and give us life.

My son, pay attention to what I say;

turn your ear to my words.

Do not let them out of your sight,

keep them within your heart;

for they are life to those who find them

and health to one's whole body. (Prov. 4:20-22 NIV)

The word of God is alive! When we speak the word of God, it is as we are speaking as God. It is His word and it cannot return void, which means it has to be done. God spoke the earth into existence: "For when He spoke, the world began. It appeared at His command." (Ps. 33:9) This clearly shows us that words have power to create and the word of God has all power over any sickness or disease. We are made in the image of God, meaning the same power that Jesus has we also have. God has given us dominion over every living thing and His word to manifest His presence and nature in our own lives and society. Once we fully realize this, then we can use the weapon of the word given to us to declare our healing. It is time to declare: "No weapon formed against me shall prevail, and God will refute every tongue that accuses me." (Is. 54:17 NIV)

If we speak, it has to happen; the key is to "speak" the word. Speak the word over your life as a defense before an affliction even appears. I urge you to speak the word and declare the healing you need in your life. The healing you are in need of may not be a physical one, but the same principle applies to mental, emotional, or relational pain; the word of God brings restoration and has power over all afflictions. Don't be like me and grasp this understanding later; grab hold of it now.

PRAYER TO SPEAK

Father God fill my mind, heart, and spirit with your Divine Word today. Cause me to speak Your Word as truth and the ultimate authority over my life, and my condition. When thoughts of unbelief and hopelessness sink in, replace them with your healing, restorative, perfect Word. Help me to bring all of my thoughts of doubt into the obedience of Christ. I will speak and declare your "logos" (word, plan, reason) over my past, present, and future circumstances, in Jesus' name, Amen.

CHAPTER THREE:
THE RAGING BATTLE
OF THE MIND

The mind is a battle zone, and the warfare that is in constant motion within the believer's mind is real and painful. If you have experienced disease of the body, you have probably also experienced the resulting side effects in your mental health as well. The two, sickness and our thought life, truly go hand in hand. The enemy may initially attack through physical affliction, but his deeper intent is to reach the mind through that affliction, thus harboring fear, doubt, and unbelief. If he can scare us enough to shake our belief in a loving and healing God, then Satan can win the war over our mental well being as well. But, we can rest assured that when we walk closely with Jesus through the fire of illness, the battle over our mind has already been won.

"For the weapons of our warfare *are* not carnal but mighty in God for pulling down strongholds, casting down arguments and every high thing that exalts itself against the knowledge of God, bringing every thought into captivity to the obedience of Christ." (2 Cor. 10:4-6 NKJV)

One of the greatest weapons of warfare God has given us is our personal faith in Jesus Christ. The Bible says that we are saved eternally "by grace through faith" (Eph. 2:8) and it also states that in the midst of spiritual warfare, faith serves as a shield, which will "quench all the fiery darts of the wicked one" (Eph. 6:16). Faith is absolutely necessary in fighting the good fight laid before us when we are battling disease in the mind and body.

It is foremost important to identify the "fiery darts" that the enemy will hurl at us in the warfare of affliction. These darts may begin with a physical attack on the body through disease and infirmity, but it is only a matter of time before those deadly arrows become embedded in our mind and our way of thinking. This is the ultimate plan of the enemy. It is not so much his goal to physically torment us, but it is through the suffering in our flesh that he can access the mind, soul, and spirit. Affliction through the flesh will eventually torment the spirit of the man if we do not put on and activate the shield of faith.

Let's look at an example of the downward spiral effect. Perhaps you have been diagnosed with a debilitating disease. The body becomes weak and vulnerable, and soon, your thought patterns are attacked through the weakness of the flesh. You might find yourself thinking thoughts that lead into the "snow-ball effect" of worry: "What if God can't heal me? What if God doesn't want to heal me? What if God is punishing me? What if I don't live to see my children grow up? What if I don't live to see my grandchildren? How will we afford to live after all of the medical expenses? How will I return to a normal life? Will I ever be normal again? How long do I have until I die? What if I am not truly saved? What if my spouse can't handle the changes in my body? What if he/she leaves me?" Before you know it, one diagnosis can skyrocket into a mess of many mental afflictions that are all illegitimately birthed from the sickness. What is a painful blow to the body can be a much more deadly blow to our spiritual life if we do not learn to recognize the dilemma, pull out the shield of faith, fight the mental attacks through the powerful name of Jesus, and speak His word over our mindset. "The thief does not come but to steal, kill and destroy. I have come that they may have life, and that they may have it more abundantly." (Jn. 10:10 NKJV)

Jesus teaches us a great lesson in the parable of the fig tree.

This lesson is just as applicable to our well being now as it was in the time he spoke it. He attests that if we ask, and BELIEVE, we will receive what we ask for. We must believe with our spiritual eyes and ears, and not those of our physical existence. If we choose to believe with that of the flesh, our mind will never come to the point of faith that Christ asks us to seek. But if we ask, and believe he can do it, then the victory has already been won, not just in our minds, but also in our physical affliction. Let's look at some examples of men and women of God who sought the Lord and did not allow the circumstances to defeat their mindset toward what God could accomplish in their personal walk and healing.

RENEE'S EXPERIENCE

Jacob's Story

I will never forget the night I finally took authority and claimed healing over a massive migraine that I experienced a month post-op my second brain surgery. My husband and I were traveling through a small oil town in West Texas. He was supposed to preach there for Father's Day, and after that we would head out to Arizona to spend a month with my family. A headache had started on the five-hour drive to Ozona, and I was sure I could control it with a few Ibuprofen, but by that evening, it had exploded into a full-blown migraine. Thankfully and surprisingly, I do not experience many migraines as a result of the surgery, but I could tell this one was a remnant of the radiation, which can cause swelling of the brain months after treatment.

That first night, I was in so much pain that I was spiritually and mentally preparing myself for death. We were in a very small town off the I-10, and I had no idea how far the nearest hospital was. Furthermore, I questioned that there would even be a neurosurgeon on staff who would accurately pinpoint the source of the torment raging in my head. After taking a heavier dose of painkillers, which always makes me feel uneasy, I finally drifted off to sleep. I awoke the next morning, but to my utter disappointment, the pain and swelling had returned, and by the second evening, I truly thought my brain was going to burst through my skull.

In previous "flare-ups" such as this, I had let fear and the lies of the enemy take a hold of me and paralyze my prayer life. In those moments of doubt and unbelief in Christ's healing power, I would not turn to prayer, as I know I should. Rather, I would rely on reassurance from medical personnel, similar stories on the Internet, and medication. There was something different about this night. This time, I had a strong conviction that the enemy had come to destroy me, and if not through my neurological health, then he would take me out through my mental health. I believe there is such a thing as being frightened to death, because the enemy is the author of fear, but God is the author of "power, love, and a sound MIND." (1 Tim. 1:7) I began to fervently pray in tongues (the language of the Spirit), to declare the word, and recite healing scriptures. And then God reminded me of Jacob. "Then Jacob was left alone; and a Man wrestled with him until the breaking of the day ...And He said 'Let me go, for the day breaks. But he (Jacob) said, "I will not let You go unless You bless me."" (Gen.32: 24, 26b NKJV)

Jacob did not simply ask the angel of the Lord to bless him, nor was he even polite or gentle in his request. Sometimes we might be up against the enemy, at the brink of physical death, and God is waiting for us to claim, profess, and wholeheartedly embrace God's healing with authority. We must be ready to commit ourselves to a place of warrior-like prayer, crying out in our desperate need for healing, "God, do not leave me this night until you bless me!"

God did not allow me to be defeated that night, although the enemy was speaking lies of deception. I remember laying flat on my face at the altar of the church we were staying in, and although my husband was by my side interceding, I knew this particular match was between me and the Lord; God was fighting for me to surrender my worry, stress, anxiety, affliction to Him. He wanted to release me from this oppression once and for all.

This is our reality when it comes to sickness. We are often like Jacob; we must encounter the Lord and have those "wrestling matches" in order to receive the healing God has for us through His Holy Spirit. When we are at the point of breaking, at a place of giving up, it is in our surrender to the Lord and our fervent prayer that God can break into our heart to bless and heal us. That night was a powerful turning point in my prayer life. I was not able to rely on doctors, medicine, or my husband for healing. The Lord will bring us to such a desperate and vulnerable place so we might rely on and fully trust in Him alone to heal, and to fight for the blessing God has already granted us, through our complete and utter faith in what he accomplished at the cross.

Needless to say, I fell asleep that night in the presence of the Almighty God on a tear-filled altar, and I awoke at the break of dawn with the indescribable peace of knowing that God had won the battle, and He had done it for me.

Jacob says in Genesis 32:30 NKJV "For I have seen God face to face, and my life is preserved." Jacob was not saved because he prayed a recited prayer, a half heartfelt request, or because someone else prayed for his relief. Rather, Jacob had to endure a one on one experience with the Almighty God to be brought to the place of blessing, a plateau of Jesus' presence and perfect peace. In your sickness, God is waiting for that struggle, for the encounter that will be the turning point in your battle against the enemy. Perhaps Jacob finally realized that God was not the enemy, and that his fighting was not to overcome the evil one, but that the battle was to overcome his own faulty mindset, and to receive the blessing that God wanted to give him. When we think thoughts of doubt, fear, and give life to words that are contrary to God's attributes and promises, we are losing the battle to our own faithless minds. But, when we learn to fight those doubts, to conquer and take captive our thoughts, we can walk in the obedience and the blessing of Jesus Christ: "...casting down arguments and every high thing that exalts itself against the knowledge of God, bringing every thought into captivity to the obedience of Christ." (2 Cor. 10:5 NKJV)

In turn, when we "cast down" our own doubts and fears, God is able to take back and reclaim our thoughts to align them with his. This is part of the blessing. But it's important that we go through the "wrestling match" in the first place to know and experience the victorious healing God has for us on the other side. Don't let yourself be taken prisoner by your own lack of faith. Continue to fight as Jacob fought, and do not relinquish any ground to the enemy, nor to your own faithlessness. God is waiting for you to come boldly to His throne and ask for your healing needs with full belief and assurance that He will grant it.

Remember Jacob's powerful prayer:

Imagine if we prayed with this kind of faith and boldness in every obstacle.

"I will not let you go (God) unless You bless me!"

LASHANDRIA'S EXPERIENCE

Hannah's Example

Throughout the bible, we can look into the testimonies of those before us and learn valuable lessons that can help us through our journey. Again, testimonies serve as a witness of the goodness of the Lord. Let's take a look at Hannah and her journey.

> There was a certain man from Ramathaim, a Zuphite from the hill country of Ephraim, whose name was Elkanah son of Jeroham, the son of Elihu, the son of Tohu, the son of Zuph, an Ephraimite. He had two wives; one was called Hannah and the other Peninnah. Peninnah had children, but Hannah had none. Year after year this man went up from his town to worship and sacrifice to the LORD Almighty at Shiloh, where Hophni and Phinehas, the two sons of Eli, were priests of the LORD. Whenever the day came for Elkanah to sacrifice, he would give portions of the meat to his wife Peninnah and to all her sons and daughters. But to Hannah, he gave a double portion because he loved her, and the LORD had closed her womb. Because the LORD had closed Hannah's womb, her rival kept provoking her in order to irritate her. This went on year after year. Whenever Hannah went up to the house of the LORD, her rival provoked her till she wept and would not eat. Her husband Elkanah would say to her, "Hannah, why are you weeping? Why don't you eat? Why are you downhearted? Don't I mean more to you than ten sons?" Once when they had finished eating and drinking in Shiloh, Hannah stood up. Now Eli the

priest was sitting on his chair by the doorpost of the Lord's house.

In her deep anguish, Hannah prayed to the Lord, weeping bitterly. And she made a vow, saying, "Lord Almighty, if you will only look on your servant's misery and remember me, and not forget your servant but give her a son, then I will give him to the Lord for all the days of his life, and no razor will ever be used on his head." As she kept on praying to the Lord, Eli observed her mouth. Hannah was praying in her heart, and her lips were moving but her voice was not heard. Eli thought she was drunk and said to her, "How long are you going to stay drunk? Put away your wine."

"Not so, my lord," Hannah replied, "I am a woman who is deeply troubled. I have not been drinking wine or beer; I was pouring out my soul to the Lord. Do not take your servant for a wicked woman; I have been praying here out of my great anguish and grief." Eli answered, "Go in peace, and may the God of Israel grant you what you have asked of him. "She said, "May your servant find favor in your eyes." Then she went her way and ate something, and her face was no longer downcast. Early the next morning they arose and worshiped before the Lord and then went back to their home at Ramah. Elkanah made love to his wife Hannah, and the Lord remembered her. So, in the course of time, Hannah became pregnant and gave birth to a son. She named him Samuel, saying, "Because I asked the Lord for him." (1Sam.1:1-20 NKJV)

There is a great wealth of knowledge and wisdom we can learn from Hannah and her testimony. Hannah was barren and physically could not produce a child. Not only did she have to suffer through the pain of not being able to get pregnant, but she watched her rival get pregnant, have the baby, and then she lived through taunting from the rival. I can imagine she faced all kinds of negative thoughts and emotions about herself, comparing herself to others, feeling inadequate, feeling hopeless like what she really wanted would never happen. Hannah had come to her breaking point and cried out to the Lord. Sometimes we have to get like Hannah and say, enough, cry out before the Lord and give it to Him. We still want to hold on and "fix it" ourselves. Sometimes God will allow us to see other people blessed with what we are waiting for, so that when it happens for us, no one else can get the glory but God because it is only He that could have done it.

Hannah had an awareness of who God is, His sovereignty, and that is what strengthened her faith. Faith comes by hearing and hearing the word of God (Rom. 10:17). Hannah had faith, she heard the word of the Lord through the prophet Eli. Hannah could genuinely worship the LORD in faith while the promise was still not yet fulfilled. This is the pattern of faith. Throughout this process, Hannah worshipped and praised the Lord, giving honor to God. Through her praise and thanksgiving, she brought glory to God through her trial. Even when the manifestation hasn't happened, yet she praises God for it in advance.

We learn that thanksgiving as a sacrifice glorifies God. Being able to recognize God's goodness, despite our circumstances, is an act of worship, which pays homage to his attributes--his grace, patience, love, and provision. Praising through the sickness, disease, trial, or whatever you are going through, is a weapon against the enemy. It takes our minds to an elevated place because we focus on God. If the enemy is after us with the battle raging in our minds, and we take our minds off the problem through praise and thanksgiving, not only does this honor God, but also it pushes back darkness and the enemy has to flee. *"It's the praising life that honors me. As soon as you set your foot on the Way, I'll show you my salvation."* (Ps. 50:23 MSG)

As soon as Hannah heard the word from Eli, she believed her prayer would be answered, she was thankful that God heard her. Hannah knew the attributes of God and His character. She knew that God was good. Hannah waited for years, and then she finally received the breakthrough. She put her faith with God's ability. When the report says no, God says yes!

I remember one night when my husband was out of town on a temporary duty assignment, and I had a Hannah moment. I was in so much pain suffering from the disease and I laid on my bed and just cried out to God. I cried and mumbled a prayer, but I knew God understood what I was saying. I had come to my breaking point where I couldn't try to be strong in my own strength anymore. I didn't have the solution that I was trying to find myself. I felt like it was the end of me trying to fix it and I just wanted to give it to God. I saw and read about the miracles of Jesus and how people were healed and delivered. I knew it could happen but wasn't seeing it in my own life. The enemy would taunt me with fear and doubt and I was trying so hard to not give in to the lies. And let's be honest, when you're experiencing extreme pain, the focus is not to praise and be thankful for it. But, for me it was a turning point on the right track to bring God's ability sovereign over my ability.

After that experience, I felt so much more peace and even though the pain was still there, I felt like I could hold on and allow God to help me. I could focus my mind on what He could do that I obviously couldn't do on my own. As time went on, I had to continue to cry out to God and keep my heart and mind in a place of praise and trusting Him as I waited for the solution to come. This ultimately helped me increase my faith in God, which is what faith is all about. The word says "faith is the substance of things hoped for and the evidence of things not seen." (Heb. 11:1 NKJV)

This is what our whole journey with the Lord is, it's faith. We have to have faith to even first believe and accept Jesus as our Lord and Savior. It takes faith to wake up everyday and go through life because someone may not live to see another day. This thing we call life is about faith, trusting and believing for something. This is how we please God, by faith, knowing it will happen even if it hasn't or we don't see how. Many times we are hoping for healing or hoping for something to turn around and get better, but hope is not faith. Hope is in the future tense and faith is in the present tense. Faith is NOW and it requires action, saying what we believe and acting like it is done. Faith comes by hearing the word of God and when we hear the word, we can put it in our mind, heart, and put it into action. The word from the Lord came to Hannah and she believed and acted on it. The goal of the enemy is to stop the word from producing in our lives. The devil wants to destroy our minds and kill our faith, but we don't have to give him any power to do that.

Maybe you are like Hannah, you have been waiting for a miracle, waiting for your healing, waiting for your break-through, waiting for a change; well my friend, don't give up and don't lose your faith in our God, because He can and will deliver on His word. Hannah received her blessing when it was time. There was something greater cultivated within her through her process of waiting and trusting the Lord. Even though the pain and suffering can feel unbearable at times, and it may feel like the healing won't happen, choose to be like Hannah and cultivate a heart and mind to praise God and stand on His word. It is through some of the most difficult times that we learn what it means to wait on the Lord and be of good courage. It takes courage to stand when the circumstances look dim. But my sister, that is the part of the journey that I believe makes us stronger.

The goal of the enemy is to cause us to lose hope, quit, give up, and die. The enemy will taunt you and point out that everyone else is being healed except you, but wait on God. Maybe you have been believing and haven't seen the manifestation yet; keep waiting on God. The enemy tries to stop us by attacking our minds with fear, doubt, worry, and any other lie that leads to depression, but focus on the truth of the word of God. "Do not conform to the pattern of this world but be transformed by the renewing of your mind. Then you will be able to test and approve what God's will is--his good, pleasing and perfect will." (Rom. 12:2 NIV)

Each day we have to renew our minds. Renewing our minds is about our relationship with Jesus and changing the way we think and how we view situations. Every day we have to come back to the place of when we first believed because the enemy won't stop coming with lies, so we can't stop renewing our mind to remind us of the truth either. The cares of life or the care of sickness will come but the word says, "Give all your worries and cares to God, for he cares about you." (1 Pet. 5:7 NLT) Give your care of the affliction to God.

As we continue to renew our minds each day, then we can grow from believing to knowing that God is who He says. God's will for us is good, and He wants us to live in a healed state not a broken one. Renewing our mind keeps our mindset focused on the solution instead of the problem.

Overall, it goes back to strengthening and developing the spirit, which will transfer to the mind, emotions, and therefore the body. In times of affliction, there really is no other way to overcome and get through it than with the power, authority, and love of God. We as believers have this power and authority over the enemy and that is what scares him the most. The enemy knows he is already defeated, and my sister, you need to know that he is defeated as well! When Jesus died on the cross for us, He eradicated all things from the enemy and set us free. Anything that you can imagine and may be going through, Jesus has set you free from. *"So if the Son makes you free, then you are unquestionably free." (Jn. 8:36 AMP)*

Even in times when you cannot handle the struggle and battle in your mind, surround yourself with people who can pray, encourage, and point you to Jesus. Surround yourself with healing prayers, scripture, positive affirmations, praise and worship, and create an atmosphere around you that will uplift your spirit and elevate your mind to focus beyond the problem. It is also important to surround ourselves with people because the enemy would want us to stay isolated, especially in times of affliction since we are in a vulnerable place mentally.

I can recall a time when I was in the emergency room after my second surgery. My small intestine stopped working, and I was in extreme pain. We didn't know what was going on and I ended up getting a tube down my nose and throat. I was tired in all areas and weak. I remember laying in the hospital bed waiting for the doctor to come in and I began to cry. I couldn't understand why that was happening after everything was supposed to be getting better; I was supposed to be in recovery. It was like I was going backwards.

My husband wasn't in the room because he left to take care of something for the kids. I was there alone and I clearly heard a voice say "you are going to die, just curse God and die." I knew it wasn't from the Lord, it definitely was the enemy. In a very vulnerable time, the enemy was influencing me to just give up and die. I very well could have died in the natural but my spirit refused to give up and I refused to listen to that negative message. I call this my "Job experience," just like Job from the Bible.

I began to say, "Lord help me, I will not die, I will not curse

God, l love you Lord." I had to turn my focus to light because darkness was trying to pull me into a pit through my mind. My spirit was stronger than my body and my mind, therefore, I know that helped me. But the mental battle was very intense and if I hadn't turned to God immediately, I could have been overtaken by it because I was in so much pain and in a fragile state of mind.

As soon as my husband came back, he prayed with me. At that point, I needed someone else to help carry me through that in prayer. The key is to go immediately to God. Your break-through in your mind, your body, and anything you need in life is in God. Not one negative thought can withstand the word and power of God. God has promised He will never leave us or forsake us! So in the worst of times, we have to know that God is with us and He can heal the physical, mental, and emotional pain we experience. "I WILL NEVER [under any circumstances] DESERT YOU [nor give you up nor leave you without support, nor will I in any degree leave you helpless], NOR WILL I FOR-SAKE or LET YOU DOWN or RELAX MY HOLD ON YOU [assuredly not]!" (Heb. 13:5 AMP)

And in the Word of God, "never" is defined as "never." There is no double standard; when God says "never," He really means it. Today, my dear sister, we invite you to surrender your negative thoughts, disbelief, hopelessness, and pain to Jesus Christ. Stand on the power of His healing touch, and guard the territory of your mind with His anointed word. Erase any words from your mind that are contrary to what God has spo-ken over you concerning your complete restoration. Do not al-low the enemy a point of entry or a final say in you overcoming sickness and death.

Remember the story of Job? As mentioned before, the dev-il's ultimate purpose in his attack upon Job was to break Him so much physically, that his spirit would also be destroyed. In this place of destruction, Satan hoped Job would deny and curse God. The devil is certainly a prowling lion, and he is cunning. Perhaps the main reason He attacks through physical affliction is because he knows if the body is weakened, this will eventually attack our spirit man. When Satan's attacks were permitted to fall upon Job, the sole purpose of these circumstances was for the devil to prove that God was wrong, that Job really did not believe or love the Lord as much as God thought.

When we are amidst physical trials or unanswered prayers and promises of God, doubt can often cause us to distrust God; some may even turn away from God because they cannot understand why a loving God would allow such pain and suffering. It is so comforting to read that Job "was blameless and upright, and one who feared God and shunned evil." (Job 1:1) This is the very first and most important fact we learn when reading the story of Job. If Job had not had these attributes, the entire book would lose its holy meaning. Although Job was "blameless" and loved the Lord, He was not protected from the attacks of the evil one. God entrusted and allowed these attacks because of Job's faithfulness. Let's wrap our minds around this idea that when such intense suffering comes our way, it is because God can entrust us to stay strong and faithful to Him even when all that we love- all comfort, all finances, all health, have been stolen from us. Job was certainly in a time of waiting. Like us, he was tempted daily to curse God for his trials and place of deep pain and brokenness. But rather than curse God, Job trusted in the character of God. He believed that God was faithful, a rewarder, a healer, a provider, no matter how he felt physically or mentally. Job succumbed to the spirit man and trusted that God was who He said he was. Rather than focusing on the circumstances, Job focused on the character and immutable attributes of the King of King. "For I know that my Redeemer lives, And He shall stand at last on the earth." (Job 19: 25)

We so often throw away our inheritance, our promise of health and healing, because we have fixed our fleshly eyes on the situation, rather than focus our spiritual eyes on God's goodness and steadfastness. He alone is our Redeemer, and when he "stands at last" it will be to complete the promises of redemption and new life He has spoken over in covenant promise.

RENEE'S EXPERIENCE

There are still days when I feel Job's story is so real in my own life. Waiting on God, and trusting in His timing, even when the present circumstance "looks" as if it will not end well. At times, like Job, we also have friends in our lives who will attempt to evaluate the situation through their "own understanding." Job's friends accused him of many shortcomings, specifically being a man who was not as blameless or holy as God himself had attested. After all, if Job was so "blameless" why would God attack him so violently and prolifically. Job's friends attempted to point out that Job had unrepented sin, and that he deserved what had been brought upon him. Throughout this book, Job argues with these friends to establish that the God he worships is not the God who had stricken him. Sadly, many times people who are well-intentioned believers will attempt to explain your suffering as a direct result of your sinfulness. In grasping for an explainable "reason" to your suffering, they draw hypothetical conclusions that are more of a comfort to themselves, perhaps than to you. Now we know that many times sin will bring negative and deadly effects upon our physical and spiritual lives, but this is not always the case. Just like Job, we must be careful and wise about who we allow to speak into our situation. Satan could have been using Job's closest friends to bring Job to such a horrible state of mind that he would curse God in the end. You, too, may have friends and family who have falsely interpreted the Word of God, as well as the prophetic word of God, in your situation.

In my walk, the aftermath of a health crisis was far more painful than prior to and during brain surgery. Several days after the surgery I was in the ER with a horrendous CSF (cerebral spinal fluid) leak that I believe was the enemy's plot to take me out, since the brain tumor itself had not destroyed me. Six months later I had radiation to the 2cm brain tumor that was left in my head because it would have been too risky to remove the entire mass. So my daily walk is often a daily battle of the mind and body, which truly affects my spirit. Aside from the trauma to my nervous system, which affects many normal functions of the body that I had taken for granted, the fear alone that I still have a tumor inside my head, and that it could potentially grow back, is often paralyzing. I have had friends tell me that perhaps God had purposefully left that tumor there so I would stay close to Him, because I was not spending time with Him the way I needed to. One friend said that if the tumor continued to grow (even after surgery and radiation) that it was because God desired a personal relationship with me and for me to draw closer to Him. Unfortunately, this is "faulty reasoning." God does not perpetrate and plague us with illness to get closer to us, but he can use this as an opportunity to grow and mature us in our walk with Him. I hope we can identify the difference in this type of thinking. In the first (that of my friend) God has afflicted us to bring about a result he desires in us. This is a strange sort of belief in a Pagan-like belief in God that God is not concerned about our suffering or pain, but that he will hurt as in order to force us into a deeper relationship. In the second, God is not the inflictor or punisher, but He does use Satan's attack as an opportunity to deepen our walk in Him. (Job 42:10)

In another scenario, I had a minister explain to me that since I was living a life of service to the Lord, that dying was no big deal, because I was doing the work of the Lord. Now while I do not entirely disagree with this, I also felt troubled in my spirit when these words were spoken to me. My thoughts raced: "And if I die, how can I continue to do the work of the Lord? Isn't this the enemy's greatest desire? For God's children to give up on the possibility of healing so that the sickness will overcome them, and their lives be cut short before the appointed time?" Even through all of his friends' harsh and false explanations, Job remained steadfast and immovable in His knowledge of the Lord. He praised Him, and believed Him at His word, and he waited for the word to pass and the blessing to manifest. Our friends may love us and mean well, but when they have incorrectly taken God's Word out of context to put their own "human" reasoning to your situation, they have belittled the power and authority of God's voice in your situation. They have managed to shrink the grandeur of God's healing grace through words of the flesh. This is why we must use discernment in our walk, and not rely on just anyone to speak to and pray over your affliction. Their words may be spoken in love, but if not aligned with God's Word, and the prophetic promises of the Holy Spirit, they can easily sow seeds of doubt and mistrust in the authenticity of God's perfect love and healing authority. This can taint our mindset and cause us to digress in our healing when we are being fed man's words, rather than the Word of God.

First and foremost, listen to and trust what God has spoken over you, and let His voice overpower any false or faulty reasoning that comes from another person. If God has told you or revealed to you that He will heal you, believe that He will, and don't let others convince you otherwise. It may take months, years, decades, but God will be faithful to His promise. In your time of waiting, trust the process, and keep your eyes focused on what awaits you at the finish line. For every measure of suffering, there will be an expiration date. It is not our job to reason and explain away the circumstances, but it is our role to wait on the Lord, to stand on His Word, to silence the voice of the enemy, and to praise God through to the fulfillment of His eternal Word. It is not a question of WHETHER God will follow through with His Word, it's only a question of WHEN it will come to pass. And as we wait, we must continue to renew our minds according to the Spirit and walk in the faith that we are indeed healed and restored. We must walk as though God has already completed the work, because He has.

Dear heavenly Father, in the name of Jesus Christ

I speak your healing and deliverance over my sister now.

I bind any thoughts that are not of you, and I replace them with the love, peace, and truth that you speak over my sister. I declare her complete healing in mind, body, and Spirit, by the powerful name of Jesus, and I loosen the chains of darkness and death that have been unlawfully declared over her life. From this day forward, she is a new and whole creation, a daughter of Jerusalem, fully healed, renewed and made alive by the power of the cross.

In Jesus' mighty name we pray. Amen.

CHAPTER FOUR:
HEALING AS A
DIVINE PROCESS

Healing is a multifaceted process in each individual, and it is the Lord's sovereign choice in how He chooses to heal the afflicted. There is no clear cut, "easy to follow" recipe to provoke the healing grace of God. God is all-powerful, El Shaddai, and in His divinely creative power, He alone can heal a person using any creative method He so chooses. It's so simple, yet we as believers can make it very complicated.

When we put stipulations and parameters on God, it does not always work out the way we desire it to, or for our best interest. We may be disappointed in the immediate results, only to find that our healing journey was a process through which God embarked to reveal himself even more miraculously in our lives, to bring the greatest glory and honor to His name. Through our walk of sickness and healing, God is clearing a path on which is written our specifically unique testimony. And when we re-read that testimony in the heavenly documents which will summarize our walk with the Lord on that great day, all will be made perfectly and unmistakably clear, and we will say "Yes and Amen." "For now we see in a **mirror**, dimly, but then face to face. Now I know in part, but then I shall know just as I also am known." (1 Cor. 13:12 NKJV)

Any normal human being would concur that miraculous, instantaneous healing would be their preferred choice when it comes to facing a life-threatening disease. We find ourselves praying for "the easy way out" because we know that God is fully able to do it, but when we pray this way, we are questioning God's sovereignty, and His ability to create an incredibly powerful testimony, a reflection of His love for us, out of something very desperate and downright evil. "And we know that **all things work together** for good to those who love God, to those who are called according to *His* purpose." (Rom. 8:28 NKJV)

Don't get me wrong; miraculous and instant acts of healing by God's hand are real and worthy of our praise. There are many examples of immediate healings by the divine touch of Jesus himself, and by the hand of the Holy Spirit working through the apostles. But, what about the times that this miraculous healing does not occur in a single moment? We must first remember that God's timing is not equal to or subject to the timing of mankind or the earthly realm in which we dwell. While we may question why God has not healed us in our timing as an instant response to a heartfelt prayer, as believers, we must accept our healing regardless of the outward appearance, or even the physical reality. We are called to stand on His word and promise that when He declared, "It is finished" indeed, it was finished. What He endured on the cross withstood the physical limitations of time, as we know it. "But He *was* wounded for our transgressions, *He was* bruised for our iniquities; the chastisement for our peace *was* upon Him, And by His stripes we are healed." (Is. 53:5 NKJV)

God's declaration of healing in the book of Isaiah affirms that no matter the duration of our physical pain and affliction, and no matter how long our physical healing takes, God has faithfully instituted his perfect healing already by the blood of Jesus. The Hebrew word "rapha" is used 33 times in the Old Testament and is translated "to make whole" both physically (in health) and spiritually. Because of His blood, we have been healed completely. God spoke this word ages ago so that we might believe and receive it today.

Because we can stand on and trust the Word of the Lord, we accept our healing regardless of the method by which He heals. It is the avenues of healing that can often sow seeds of unbelief and doubt in the faith of the believer. We may ask, "God, you said I am healed, but I don't see the results. Why am I not seeing the full manifestation? If I am healed, why do I need to see a doctor? Why did I have to have surgery? Why am I in the hospital?" The physical limitations of our mind and our flesh will work in contrast to the will and finished word of the Father. Our limited understanding will question God's goodness and faithfulness in the midst of the healing journey we are on. God is both sovereign and faithful; He is a creative Father who will work in every situation to reveal His glory in our healing process. We must come to a place where we fully surrender our lack of understanding to His divine and sovereign hand, and in the meantime, continue to trust and declare the Word over our affliction.

Our God is a healer; in Hebrew, He is Jehovah Rapha, the healer. Our God is also the creator, and the steward of immeasurable creative possibilities, "Elohim" the divine creator. If God is both "Healer" and "Creator" that also makes Him the "Creative Healer." We have been in the ministry long enough to understand that ignorance of the Word, and therefore of God, is a sad weakness in the church today. God's people have unknowingly put limitations on God's creative power. Why? Just because man cannot fathom other methods and avenues through which God moves, in our own natural understanding, does not mean that they in fact do not exist. God is not only the creator, but also the initiator of infinite possibilities. He is the God of what man thinks is "impossible."

LASHANDRIA'S EXPERIENCE

I had always understood that God was a healer, but throughout the many years of struggling with ulcerative colitis, I never realized the power of God to heal me. I had not set my faith to receive healing and I just struggled through with disease. I prayed for healing and honestly, I begged for healing, but it wasn't until the sickness had me at the lowest point where I had come to the understanding of God as healer. I learned more about scriptures that specifically were for healing and how every sickness and disease was from the devil. I believed for instant healing as that is what I had always seen or heard of when it came to healing. But as I waited, I realized that God is creative in how He speaks, moves, heals, and in how He does everything. God will use whatever and whoever He chooses to get to us the blessing we need.

My colon was medically in the worst condition that it could have ever been in beyond physical repair. I had come to a crossroads where I had to make a decision whether to have surgery to remove it or keep it in and continue to suffer and keep myself at risk of cancer. I was told to pray about it and continue to speak the word of God over my body. Some people were not sure whether surgery was the right option because the question was whether I had believed and done all I could do to wait for instant healing.

It's this perspective that gets believers and unbelievers stuck, because God's goodness is not based on what we do. God is good regardless and He wants to bless us, He wants us healed, He loves us. Our healing is not based on our acts of striving to make it happen. God's goodness is not based on our righteousness and what those people didn't understand was that I had waited and struggled with this for many years. Now I was at the point of being in serious danger and having to make a major decision. Sometimes people will try to give you their opinion but God's word and will for us doesn't require man's opinion. When God says, "this is the way," obedience must come first before what others may think or even our own fears.

All it takes is faith the size of a mustard seed. All we have to do is believe and receive our healing by faith. Now, however that healing comes is up to God and sometimes God will require us to take a step of faith and put action with our faith to receive the healing. If it is an instantaneous miracle that is great, but if it is through surgery that is great as well, the key is to receive the healing. By the stripes of Jesus, we are already healed anyway.

My husband and I prayed one night after a long struggle with pain and God showed us to move forward with the surgery. It was a scary decision for me because I didn't want to go through surgery, who does? There are so many risks involved and this was major surgery, not to mention the life changes after it. But I knew that God told me to do this and He was with me. I know now more than ever that God used the surgeons and surgery as a tool to bring my healing. God connected me with the right surgeon who cared and walked me through the process just as God would. God uses many avenues to heal us and it very well may be a miracle or it can come through the hands of doctors. If at the end of the journey, we come out better than we were before, our brokenness is restored, that's healing and it is all attributed to the grace, power, and love of God.

I recognize God as my healer and His healing for me through surgery. God uses doctors and their hands to enact his plans in people's lives. I had to take a step of faith and get the surgery to receive my healing. God removed something in me that no longer worked for my good and used surgery to work for my good. God is the divine and creative healer.

"Every good thing given and every perfect gift is from above; it comes down from the Father of lights [the Creator and Sustainer of the heavens], in whom there is no variation [no rising or setting] or shadow cast by His turning [for He is perfect and never changes]." (James 1:17 AMP)

Our whole walk with God is about faith. Faith is the substance of things hoped for and the evidence of things not seen. Faith is believing without having all the answers, it's trusting, and it requires action. We have to actively engage in faith, so it's not enough to just believe I am going to be healed but to take action as if I am already healed. This concept became real to me after my surgery. When it comes to receiving our healing, we have a responsibility to do just as much as believe. We see this in examples with Jesus:

Jesus healed the man with the shriveled hand by commanding, "stretch out your hand" (Mt. 12:13)

Peter ministered healing to the paralytic man at the temple gate by saying "In the name of Jesus Christ of Nazareth, walk." (Acts 3:6-7)

Peter ministered healing to Aeneas, the paralytic of Lydda saying, "Jesus Christ heals you. Get up and roll up your mat." (Acts 9:34)

Paul ministered healing to a man that was lame from birth by speaking, "Stand up on your feet!" (Acts 14:10)

In each of these examples, we find that the person had to take action in some way to receive their healing. They put their belief with action and that is faith. Faith moves mountains and can move the giants in our life. This is also where the word of God comes in as well because faith comes by hearing and hearing the word of God. Our capacity for faith increases the more we take in the word.

Jesus replied, "Have faith in God [constantly]. I assure you and most solemnly say to you, whoever says to this mountain, 'Be lifted up and thrown into the sea!' and does not doubt in his heart [in God's unlimited power], but believes that what he says is going to take place, it will be done for him [in accordance with God's will]. For this reason I am telling you, whatever things you ask for in prayer [in accordance with God's will], believe [with confident trust] that you have received them, and they will be given to you. (Mark 11:22-24 AMP)

All of this is a part of healing because miracles don't cause faith, the word of God causes faith, and faith causes belief and action, and that causes healing. This is what I learned about having surgery. Would it have been my first choice, probably not, but God was telling me to put action with my belief and receive my healing. God doesn't tell us to do something we can't do and it's not up to us or anyone else to judge it. Maybe for someone else the action will be different but the key thing is to seek God on what the action is, believe, and receive the healing. Maybe your healing will come instantly, and it definitely can because in the name of Jesus, we were given authority to speak to circumstances and diseases and call miracles into existence!

RENEE'S EXPERIENCE

"Jesus looked at them intently and said, "Humanly speaking, it is impossible. But with God everything is possible." (Matt. 19:26 NLT)

This realization did not manifest in my life until after having brain surgery. My limited understanding of God as my healer was also one in which I had put "requirements" on God, rather than letting him move in His creative manner. What were my requirements? Well, to be quite honest, I wanted instantaneous, miraculous healing. I wanted it now! And many brethren at the time, all with good intentions, wanted the same. I am thankful for the prayers and intercession from my brothers and sister in Christ. There were some that prayed for me, both in person and over the phone, which called for divine and instant healing. There is nothing wrong with this.

And there were others who prayed for this same thing, and when it did not happen, instead of laying it in the hands of our almighty Healer, placed the blame and shame on the one who was not healed. Maybe you have been in my shoes, beloved friend. You were prayed over and expectant of the miracle, and when God said "Wait, I have a better plan" man said, "What? You didn't have enough faith, therefore God could not heal you." But little do these brethren understand that our God is limitless in his creative power. He is the God who put mud on a blind man's eyes to activate sight. He allowed Lazarus to die and lay in a tomb for three days before resurrecting his dear friend. Were Martha and Mary doubtful? Yes! They were doubtful and judgmental of Jesus' choice to prolong the miracle. And what did God mean to produce in the first-hand witnesses of this miracle? Faith, faith, and faith. If God wanted to heal everyone in the same manner, he would. That's easy for him. It's not that God cannot do it. God does not heal for His own sake, or to build His faith. God heals to bring glory to His name, and to build the faith inside the hearts of those who believe He can. Jesus said to her, "Did I not say to you that if you would believe you would see the glory of God?" (John 11:40 NKJV)

It all comes down to one thing; God always works to bring glory to His name. We Christians have tried to develop a formula for healing (and it may look something like this: laying on of hands/prayer from other believers + sick person believes = instantaneous miraculous healing, but God is not a God of predictability and formulaic power. We can accept and believe in our healing, but we must leave the method up to God.

I had one person say to me a week before the craniotomy, "I admire you for choosing surgery. Other Christians would not have for fear they would be judged by others as faithless." This truly grieved by spirit. My friend was right, and he certainly meant well by the comment, but it is a bleak and very true reality in the church today. It reminds me of the joke many pastors have shared that talks about the man who was drowning in the middle of the ocean. He prayed for help to be sent, and when the Lord sent a helicopter to rescue him, the man refused because it was not directly from God. What happened? He drowned. And when he finally saw God face to face, God asked, "Why did you refuse my help? Didn't you see I had answered your request and sent you a helicopter?"

When I was first diagnosed with a brain tumor, many of my faithful friends and family in Christ were praying for an immediate and miraculous healing to occur by the hand of Jesus. I have to admit, I was praying for this as well. A good friend and sister in Christ who lived too far to visit me wanted to pray for my healing over the phone, and I hopefully accepted her offer. As she prayed I was surprised to see a vision of God's hand reaching into my skull and pulling out a crown of thorns (the size of the actual tumor) that had been embedded in my brain. This was very similar to a vision I had experienced 10 years prior, when I was experiencing heart pains, and God reached into my heart and replaced it with a renewed heart of flesh. The vision God gave me of the tumor wrapped in a crown of thorns was just the hint of hope that I so desperately needed at that time.

I was scheduled for major brain surgery/craniotomy in two

weeks. As much as I begged the Lord to heal me in that moment, the Holy Spirit was revealing to me that I was not going to be healed by an instantaneous miracle. God would heal me (this He had already confirmed in the vision, which was confirmed in the Word of God), but it would be through his methods of intervention, and on His calendar. It is difficult to trust when you are in the middle of the storm, but the Bible says that His Word will not return void: "My word will not return to me empty, but will accomplish what I desire." (Isa. 55:11 NIV) So when God gives us a vision, we must believe it and receive it as truth, no matter what fear and doubt might be telling us. The enemy is always prowling around; searching for an open door of doubt to creep in God's time is not subject to the laws of nature, to the bondage of the flesh. While my mind was pleading for a supernatural miracle, God was speaking to my heart and telling me to "wait and patiently believe" that His Word would be accomplished.

I knew from the beginning stages that I must go through this surgery, but many of my friends and family, my husband especially, had a difficult time accepting this as God's plan. In their heart of hearts, they prayed vigorously that the tumor be removed before the surgery. I felt their prayers, and I was blessed and empowered by their intercession, and although I believed God heard every single heartfelt prayer, I knew they would not be answered in the timing they, nor I, had anticipated. As thankful as I am for these brothers and sisters in Christ, these prayer warriors who poured their hearts out to the Lord on my behalf, I kept hearing Jesus' prayer in the Garden:

"He went a little farther and fell on His face, and prayed, saying, 'O My Father, if it is possible, let this cup pass from Me; nevertheless, not as I will, but as You will." (Matt. 26:39 NKJV)

And so, God's story He had written for my healing journey included the use of other willing vessels to glorify His name in the process. God decided to use a neurosurgeon to be His hands as he directed this brave physician through an immensely risky and serious 10-hour surgery. My husband said when Dr. Robinson shook his hand at the culmination of the operation, he felt like he was shaking hands with an angel. Can God use doctors to help in his healing process? I believe so. Was it because I didn't have enough faith to be healed on the spot? That is what some religious people might have you believe. Every healing is different, every story is unique, and God has a plan and purpose for the way in which he will manifest the healing. It could happen in 1 minute, it could take 20 years. He is perfecting in us the faith to truly believe with all our mind, soul, and strength that He will bring the healing to completion in His time, and in His uniquely beautiful way.

It can be tempting to ask ourselves, "Why didn't God heal me miraculously? If he performed such miracles in the Bible, why couldn't this happen to me?" But instead ask, "What is God speaking to me through His Spirit while I am on the path to complete healing?" If I were to give an honest answer the question, "Would your faith in Jesus have grown stronger, and your story a living testimony to His work if you had been healed through one intense prayer?" My answer would sadly be, "No." In my human weakness, I would have praised God in that moment, shared my story, and forgotten about it a year later. But rather, God gave me a different story, one in which I had to trust His divine will every waking moment of every day I lived in the aftermath of two major brain surgeries. And here is yet another twist to my testimony, the tumor was not completely removed due to the risk of major complications and nerve damage that could have resulted. God allowed my neurosurgeon to leave a pea-size residual piece of the tumor, and I live with that reminder every day. At first, it was a thorn in my side, but now I see God's purpose in leaving it there. It is teaching me to completely rely on HIs strength, and furthermore, speak the Word of God continually. I still believe I am healed, even when the MRI's show it is still there, because I know what the Lord showed me from the start, and I know what His word says, "He sent out his word and healed them, snatching them from the door of death." (Ps. 107:20 NLT)

This is where I must meet God on my path, and allow my faith to grow more powerful than my fear. We choose to declare the Word over our lives, rather than demand our will over God's. Pray and speak scriptures of healing while you are on the road there, and God will show up in a strong and incredible way. His desire is for us to desire Him, and we can't truly desire Him unless our life depends on it. God wants to use us in our time of physical infirmity to rebuild us, and to testify to his healing power moving within us to others who are doubtful. His timing is not our timing; it is the timing of his kingdom and his perfect will.

"For you were born for such a time as this. (Esther 4:14 NKJV)

PRAISE AS A PATHWAY TO HEALING

How can we stay strong in the Lord as we endure and wait upon the physical manifestation of our healing? Worship is one of the greatest weapons of warfare in fighting the battle over our minds. The enemy wants to hold us captive and even tempts us into believing that God does not desire our healing, and this can institute unforeseen bondage over our affliction. Satan, who was once a great musician and worshipper himself, will venture to steal the song in our heart, thus bringing our belief for healing into captivity. So in the times when we are most desperate to see the end result of our healing, it is imperative to enter into an attitude and atmosphere of praise. Your words and songs of worship will kill every minute speck of doubt and unbelief that the enemy has sown. The mindset of a renewed and healed heart comes with the physical act of worship. Our words have the "power to speak life and death." (Prov. 18:21) and what better way to speak life than through acts of praise and worship to our healing God, Jehovah Rapha.

ENCOURAGEMENT FOR YOU

Sister, trust that your prayers for healing have already been answered. And his answer is always "Yes and amen." Don't allow other people, circumstances, or the enemy to doubt that you are healed because of the physical consequence your body is subject to in the law of this world. Declare what God already won for you in His kingdom, and that is your complete wholeness in mind, body and spirit. He won it all, and no guile of the evil one can snatch that promise from you. God wants to use you as a testimony of his infinite grace and healing. Instead of people feeling sorry for you, show people that you are already a victor because He reigned victorious on that cross.

Whatever the illness or brokenness that you are experiencing, remember that God is a creative healer, and that means he can use any method He wants- prayer, surgery, medicine, and trusting in Him. If you pray for healing, and God heals through the hands of a gifted surgeon, then praise God! You know it was not the surgeon's power that saved you, it was Jesus. If you are suffering from unrelenting pain and there is a medicine that helps ease that pain, praise God! He has offered you some rest from the discomfort until your physical body is completely restored in heaven. Maybe you have received the news that you have an aggressive form of cancer, which requires a vigorous series of chemotherapy treatments. Do you refuse the treatment, or do you accept it knowing that when you are healed, you will give praise to the Lord, not to the chemo?

Jesus came to give us an abundant life. "Through him all things were made; without him nothing was made that has been made. In him was life, and that life was the light of all mankind." (John 1:3-4 NIV) It is through Jesus that we have life and He chooses the path He gives us to life, it is our proper response to accept Him and allow Him to take care of the details.

We want to challenge you to pray a simple prayer of release and submission to God at this moment. Release to Him any preconceived ideas of how you should be healed and allow Him to be your "creative healer" and surprise you with His methods. Relinquish the limitations and parameters you have given God, and ask Him to heal in His divinely unique way. You will not be disappointed!

CHAPTER FIVE:
THE AFTERMATH

Sometimes we all need a push, maybe even a catapult, to project us into our purpose and calling. God can use just about any unfavorable circumstances to give us a helpful push into His divine plan for our lives. Painful as it is, the heartache and suffering we endure from health afflictions may just be the push we need in our lives to fulfill plans that have been sitting, lifeless and dormant; unfulfilled callings in the life of the believer is a travesty. We must strive for the purpose and the upward call that we were created for. God expects nothing less, nor should we desire less when we walk in the grace of God and the power of His Spirit.

Illness and near-death experiences can be used by God to rekindle a plan He has already placed on our hearts. As believers, we can fall into routine, and pattern our lives in a way we think is following the call of God. This can include our daily devotions, prayer time, parenting habits, work responsibilities, and roles as wives. In all the hustle and bustle we can stop listening to the voice of God in our hearts, especially when it comes to divine plans.

When God first gives us a vision of a plan he desires us to fulfill for His kingdom, we are excited, eager, and passionate to walk in that dream. Life can quickly get in the way and prevent our Kingdom focus.

LASHANDRIA'S EXPERIENCE

"And the God of all grace, who called you to his eternal glory in Christ, after you have suffered a little while, will himself restore you and make you strong, firm and steadfast." (1 Pet. 5:10 NIV

One thing I didn't realize until later was the effect of the surgery and the process after everything was done. It took a lot out of me and some days it was draining because of the various issues I had to overcome from wearing the ostomy bag, navigating through the pain, the struggle of seeing myself differently, going back into the hospital because my intestine stopped working, and many other factors. The process of recovery took some time with a lot of bumps in the road and a whole lot of adjusting and healing.

I now have a j pouch and though it is not "normal" and it has its own issues, my quality of life has improved significantly. I do however have frequent trips to the bathroom with embarrassing noises, occasional butt burn and irritation especially depending upon the food I eat, an occasional achy stomach and gas pain. I don't have the active symptoms that I once had with the inflammation in my body, but the impact of this disease is still real to me every day when I look at my scars. There is always the fear that the enemy tries to bring that something is wrong with my intestine or it will stop working. If I experience any pain or symptoms like I used to, then fear creeps in that something bad is happening to my body. The trauma of the past is there to question if this is going to happen again, if the doctor missed something with the diagnosis, or is it really healed? But, this is all a lie from the devil and he plays upon the mind. That's why it's important to heal the mind and emotions as well as the body. I had to release the fear that I was going to be sick again. Fear is just false evidence that seems to be real, but it absolutely is not! I had to use the word of God and positive affirmations to help me realize that what happened to me was okay because God turned it around for my good and I was in a better place.

This sickness took a piece of me and as time goes on, I am learning to gain it back. In the recovery phase, the enemy wants us to focus on the negative aspects such as the pain or the doubts and fears of what if. But one thing I know that helped me to get through recovery was to focus on the goodness of God. I had to keep my mind and heart fixed on the fact that I was alive, I wouldn't suffer anymore from ulcerative colitis, I didn't have cancer, I had so much love and support around, and this phase that I was in was temporary. In any type of situation where we are waiting on healing, the wrong response is fear. The wrong response is to turn away from God; in fact, it is most crucial to draw closer to God and things of God as we walk through the trial. We have to keep our focus on Jesus and His supernatural power to bring us through. Our pain has an expiration date and we are not to make a covenant with it because it is temporary.

"Weeping may endure for a night, but joy cometh in the morning." (Psalm 30:5 KJV)

Once I was able to, I started focusing more on my health and fitness by working out and staying active. I am so thankful that God led me to have the surgery and even with all the ups and downs of the recovery, I can truly say my body is healed. I am in a much better and restored place than I was before. I still have to take responsibility for my health and make wise choices with what I eat and I have to preserve the one intestine that I have left. In the natural, I am susceptible to other autoimmune diseases but I refuse to accept that. My immune system is susceptible to be weaker but I refuse to accept that. I live by the spirit not by the flesh or natural experience.

Honestly, there are still days, few in number where I don't feel my best. It all depends on if I ate something that doesn't sit right with my intestine or if air gets trapped inside. I have to fight against other issues that came from having ulcerative colitis like joint pain. I still have to face the aftermath of the disease and surgery, watch what I eat and my stress levels. I am susceptible to dehydration, easily getting sick, and even inflammation of the j pouch.

Nevertheless, I choose life, health, and the healing that Jesus died on the cross to give me thousands of years ago. It is because of the blood that you and I are here today, and we are healed, set free, and redeemed. I have the power to overcome and so do you. I choose healing and the belief that God has healed me and given me my life back. He has restored me to a greater level not only physically but spiritually also. I choose to live my life by the spirit, in peace and not in worry or fear. If worry or fear do creep in, then I know how to overcome it and it has to be a consistent practice of speaking in faith what I want to see manifest. We have to continually learn to direct our words and actions toward faith in spite of fear.

"The mind governed by the flesh is death, but the mind governed by the Spirit is life and peace." (Rom. 8:6 NIV)

Many struggle and live with this disease everyday just as I did and I am praying for those warriors. The only way to control it is through medication. But if the symptoms get worse and the medications stop helping, then surgery is the only way to remove the disease in the natural or through miraculous healing from the Lord. Once it has affected the whole colon it's quite extreme and severe. The disease eats away the lining of the colon.

In my case, my whole colon was severely affected and damaged. The lower part was strictured, which means it was narrow. This made it very difficult for stool to come out and made trips to the bathroom long and painful. If I didn't have the stricture, I probably would have never had the surgery and would still be living with chronic ulcerative colitis yet still believing and declaring the manifestation of my healing. I believe my journey to healing would have still happened but would look different. I truly believe and know that it is not God's will for us to be sick and in pain. I believe that complete healing is possible and my journey may have looked different but I would have still reached that result through faith and the goodness of God.

"And we know that in all things God works for the good of those who love him, who have been called according to his purpose." (Rom. 8:28 NIV)

Let's be honest... pain and suffering are miserable and no one voluntarily signs up to experience it. But in this life whether we are believers or not, we will go through some things that cause us pain. Through that pain can come some of the greatest things we could ever "birth." What good "fruit" has your pain produced inside of you that needs to be shared to HELP others? God uses our pain as a launching pad for our calling and purpose. In fact, this is how the ministry of She Overcame and this book were born, through our pain and affliction. Blessings can come from storms.

RENEE'S EXPERIENCE

"Consider it pure joy, my brothers and sisters, whenever you face trials of many kinds, because you know that the testing of your faith produces perseverance." (James 1:2-3 NIV)

This entire process has produced in me more than what

I could have ever imagined and it's not over yet; there is still more to learn. God will truly take what was meant for evil and turn it around for our good. Now, I can stand and tell others-you can make it.

Months before the discovery of an acoustic neuroma, I was working as a long-term substitute teacher in a public school, hoping to secure a full-time position at the same school for the following year. It was a difficult school, with hard to reach students and an unsupportive principal. I was physically, mentally, and spiritually exhausted. In the evenings I was teaching ballet, so altogether I was working over 40 hours a week. My daughter, Alegra was only 3 years old, and we were trying for another child, which was only resulting in early pregnancy loss. I had so much going on I couldn't even begin to consider the vision God had for me. The devil had a good hold on me through my weaknesses: work and pleasing others.

In April 2017, I had a dream that shook me up in a frightening way. God has often spoken to me through prophetic dreams, so when I had this one, I was ready to listen. In my dream, my left side of my head was being tested with a sort of "detector" and as it ran over the area where I had been experiencing paresthesia in my face, it began to beep with rapid warning sounds. I then heard the doctor tell me with great worry, that I had a tumor. I woke up in a sweat and only a few weeks later, was prompted to get the MRI that would reveal the illness. Now I am not saying that God gave me this tumor to give me a reality check. But I do believe that he can use these circumstances to move us back on the path he intended us to follow. There is nothing like a confrontation with death that will redirect our lives to the original vision and Kingdom purpose God built into our DNA before we were even conceived. "The counsel of the Lord stands forever, the plans of His heart to all generations." (Ps. 33:11 NKJV)

The plans of God's heart must prevail over our own plans. We will find ourselves running in circles like Moses and the Israelites if we fail to seek and listen to the voice of God in our lives. I am thankful for the setback because it accelerated my obedience to God's purpose in my life and forced me to slow down and reevaluate my purpose in Him. Although I thought I was working for the Lord, I was prioritizing my life on my terms, not His. It was easier to fall into the routine of what I had always done in life, rather than step out in boldness and claim the dreams God had reserved for me as His child.

Don't be discouraged, dear sister. You may be going through a serious, life-threatening illness and wonder if God has forgotten you. But this could be farther from the truth. He loves you and through the pain and suffering, He is calling you to rise up and step, with authority, into the original word God spoke over your life when He first called you. And because of what you have suffered in disease, broken relationships, and spiritual battles, God is asking you to stand with His authority in your distinct unique calling. In the aftermath of the pain and suffering, instead of asking "Why me God?" Yes, I asked God this question every day for two years) we can ask, "How can my story bring you glory?"

I have often thought of where I would be if I had not fallen ill. I don't believe I would be walking with freedom in God's plan and purpose. I would still be making excuses about being too busy with work and family to pursue the goals God had put on my heart: developing a healing dance ministry, writing a book, and fulfilling my role as wife and mother.

Every time I feel the return of symptoms from the tumor (and this is, quite honestly, most days) I have a choice to speak over my wellbeing in the name of Jesus, or to wallow in worry about returning conditions and self-pity. I wish I could tell you that every time I suffer I speak in faith, but all too often I am bound by my own weakness of doubt, instead looking at my situation with the eyes of my flesh. On the days when I turn to the Lord and speak His word over my pain, I feel an incredible sense of power in Jesus' name, and His peace that surpasses all understanding strengthens and sustains me.

Let me provide an example. In my first months of recovering from brain surgery, I was paranoid and downright annoyed at every new symptom that arose. My first "go-to" in authority would be my neurosurgeon and the physician's assistant who was present at the operation. Whether it was a phone call or text, I would contact these experts hoping that their advice or diagnosis would give me a sense of calm and assure me that these "aftermath" conditions were normal. As wonderful and amazing as this neurological team was, I never felt that their words gave me much peace or comfort in my situation. I often received responses that what I was feeling was not related to the surgery (when it in fact was) or that if there was regrowth we would find out in my next MRI (six months later). Hmmm, not exactly the solace I was seeking, and most often I felt worse than before I contacted them.

What I learned in my time of recovery is an incredible strength and intimacy that arises when we learn how to speak God's word over our lives in a season of physical attack and spiritual warfare. God's word commands us to, "Take every thought captive to the obedience of Christ."

We can only accomplish this by reading God's Word, and then speaking it over our condition. When we can develop an intimate relationship with the Lord through His Word, we are also commanding the authority of His healing power over our debilitation. A relationship with God through His divine word will:

1. Renew the mind

2. Control our thoughts, especially when they are filled with doubt

3. Control our tongue to speak the words of Jesus over our lives

ACTION STEPS

What is the purpose God has placed on your heart? Ponder it, meditate on His Word, revive the vision He gave you when you first gave your heart to Him. Let your trial be a fire starter that will catapult you into the perfect will of God. Ezekiel spoke of the dry bones coming to life. We challenge you to write down a few of these "dry bones" that need to be revived and born again in your walk with the Lord. Then pray over them and ask the Lord to give you the strength, wisdom, and Holy Spirit power to bring those bones back to life:

And He said to me, "Son of man, can these bones live?"

So I answered, "O Lord God, You know."

Again He said to me, "Prophesy to these bones, and say to them, 'O dry bones, hear the word of the Lord! Thus says the Lord God to these bones: "Surely I will cause breath to enter into you, and you shall live. (Ezek. 37:3-5 NKJV)

When God instructed Ezekiel to "prophesy to these bones" he was giving his followers in the future a prophetic word as well. Our words hold great power in His kingdom. It is for this reason that we are called to "prophesy" to that which is dead, in essence, to speak over the diseases in our lives to bring about healing and renewed life. When health setbacks bind us physically, it is God's word spoken over our lives that will sustain us in the weakness of our flesh, and this restores us to a state of renewal and healing in Christ. There are many accounts of Jesus speaking healing over the sick, the lame, lepers, and even the dead. He didn't pray a dramatic, lengthy, sophisticated, or poetic prayer to His Father; he simply spoke with boldness and authority, knowing His Father would hear and respond, *"So I will prove to you that the Son of Man has authority on earth to forgive sins." Then Jesus turned to the paralyzed man and said, 'Stand up, pick up your mats, and go home." (Luke 5:24 NLT)*

What happened next, the man stood up, picked up his mat, and went home praising God. You may feel the burden and weightiness of your sickness, but we must not let the physical pain and suffering distract us from what God has already done. If it is a heart condition, speak to the heart. If it is a mental affliction, speak to the mind. If it is cancer, speak to the cells. God the Father showed us a perfect and sinless example through Jesus Christ, His son on how to exercise authority over these afflictions. Speak, open your mouth, and let His word take captive the pain in your life.

ENCOURAGEMENT FOR YOU

When you are feeling the weight and torture of physical pain, say…

"He was bruised for our transgressions, And by His stripes I am healed."

When you are feeling conflicted with feelings of doubt that the Lord can heal you, say….

"With man it is impossible, but with God, all things are possible."

When Satan tempts you with thoughts of hopelessness and loss of trust in God's omniscient power, say...

"I am more than a conqueror through Him that loves me."

When you feel alone in your sickness, and it seems as if no one understands your pain, say...

"He will be with me, even to the end of this age."

When the fear of physical death creeps into your mind, say...

"Though my outward body is perishing, my inward body is being renewed every day."

The scriptures offer an endless source of His Word to declare in the midst of your battle. The prayers and comfort of the body of Christ are important but will never fulfill the emptiness and hopelessness the way God can through His word. Especially if you have been actively involved in His ministry, you may be very accustomed to praying over people for healing but when we ourselves have been attacked in our health, we must declare and believe the same words we have spoken over others.

Challenge yourself this day to conquer negative, fear-filled thoughts by speaking His word over yourself. Every time a thought of doubt and unbelief creeps into your heart, begin to speak His Word. Write down scriptures that will help you remember His promises. Instead of seeking the "right" words from family, friends, spouses, doctors, and people who really do mean well, fill your mind and renew your mind with His word.

CHAPTER SIX:
FAMILY MATTERS

The effects of our journey to healing are far-reaching, extending beyond our personal battle toward recovery. When Jesus spoke of the body needing each part to function, He described an organism that both rejoiced and suffered when other "members" were going through tough times. A true test of familial love and friendships is going through a life-changing diagnosis. We very quickly realize that though we may feel painfully alone in our struggle, in actuality, we are not. God has already positioned and surrounded us with the family and friends who will lift us up and walk with us during this time, and after. "Rejoice with those who rejoice, and weep with those who weep." (Rom. 12:15 ESV)

Although sickness can sometimes blind us in our weakness, once we begin to emerge from the darkness of those times, God reveals to us that we were and are never alone. We begin to awaken to the spiritual support system God began to put in place even before our diagnosis.

LASHANDRIA'S EXPERIENCE

When I look at my husband, I see a man who kept his covenant of promise through sickness or in health. I see a man who absolutely loves me and stood by me in strength and patience. This man fought for me in prayer and worship and he held down our home. This man took care of me on so many levels and was a strong support in this journey. If you ever have anyone like this in your life, cherish the relationship and honor that person. Never take them for granted and let them know how much you appreciate and love them. I can recall the numerous times my husband, Vito, would lift me from the bed, put on my pants, and even tie my shoe when I was severely weak. In fact, I can recall how he lovingly fixed me breakfast each morning before getting himself and the kids ready for work and school. I remember how he drove me to each doctor's appointment and each physical therapy session. We still think about it and chuckle at how I would walk out of physical therapy sessions and pretend to jog for only a few feet and get winded and tired. Every time I experienced excruciating pain in the middle of the night, Vito was up right there by my side. It is trials like this that test your marriage and relationship and it can prove to strengthen the bond or hinder it. I am thankful that this trial has strengthened our bond and emphasized for me the love of God through my husband.

One of the challenging aspects of this whole journey for me was motherhood and sickness. We have three kids and during this time, they were two, five, and eight years old. My son started kindergarten, and that whole year I was extremely sick. I was not able to engage as I normally would with helping him with homework, reading, and the foundation of his education. He struggled with reading and I blamed myself because I was sick and not able to help him. Now I know that was a lie the enemy was using, but I still felt bad. I can say that he has progressed and is doing much better in reading now in the fourth grade, thank you Jesus! But I dealt with guilt from not being present like I wanted to be or would have been if I weren't sick. Going through this, I felt a flood of emotions and thoughts including anger. It is okay to be angry but remember to be angry and sin not.

"In your anger do not sin: Do not let the sun go down

while you are still angry." (Eph. 4:26 NIV)

I also didn't want my kids to see me cry in pain or feel like they were missing something. I believe the support of my husband and the environment of love helped the kids still have structure and "normalcy." But I think it still affected them to see their mommy sick and the way we all handled it was by the grace of God.

Being a mom is one of the most challenging responsibilities by itself, let alone add sickness into the equation, but I thank God for my family. My family was also a strong support for me that I couldn't have gone through this without them. My mom, dad, brother, my aunts, uncles, and all my family and friends helped in some way. Some came down and helped me with the kids and housework duties from cooking to cleaning. Some helped me with personal hygiene and medications. Some were prayer warriors and encouragers.

One of the hardest moments for me as a mother during all of this was when my youngest daughter, who was 2 years old at the time, went to Houston for two and a half months with my aunt. My aunts had come to help me when I was sick and saw that I couldn't physically take care of my daughter. I could barely take care of myself. During that time, I didn't have the energy and I was in so much pain, not to mention I was taking a lot of medicine and I mostly slept all day because of it. I was also in the middle of graduate school and had to complete writing assignments online in my bed on medication and sometimes in pain. I wasn't going to stop school, I couldn't stop school, so I wrote papers while I was highly medicated and with the help of the Holy Spirit.

I was an emotional and physical mess. I couldn't drive to take my daughter to the daycare program or get out of bed to play with her. So, we let her go with my aunts because it was the best choice to make and I knew she was safe and would be taken care of. It was hard and I remember sitting in the bathtub crying because I didn't want to let her go but I knew I had to. I needed that time to rest and get better. I am thankful that my aunt wanted to do that, and I appreciate the love shown to my daughter and me. It's this kind of support that helps to get you through difficult times.

I also remember my mother in law always saying that she had me on the prayer list at her church and people were always asking how I was doing. I had a longtime friend who I consider to be my brother, call and check on me frequently. It was an important part of my healing not just physically, but in my soul, to know that I have people in my life that were there when I needed them the most. They all were a blessing and a huge part of my healing and recovery. It is peaceful to the mind and spirit to know that you have people around you in your corner that truly care about you and support you. I am so thankful to them and will never forget their love.

God can take something bad and bring good out of it. This experience brought us closer as a family, created relevance and understanding of prayer for my kids, and produced in us greater levels of the fruit of the spirit. For me, this was the true meaning of it not being a "solo fight." So many times when we face affliction, it can feel lonely. It's like something only you are experiencing because it is directly affecting you, and to a certain degree you do feel the most impact of it, but it also affects those around you. For family and friends that truly care, it has an impact on them as well. If they are there to help and pray, then it is not a solo fight. We never have to fight alone, anyway, because we have a God who never leaves us and will fight on our behalf. We don't have to go through it or come out of it alone.

My sister pray for God to bring people around you and in your life that will help restore your healing. Unfortunately, sometimes marriages and family relationships suffer because of the hardship of the trial, but relationships are very important to God and it is His intention that our relationships with others be unified. Many times, broken relationships can wreak havoc on our mind, emotions, and body. All of these are interconnected, and this is why it is important to restore relationships that need healing and have people in your life that will be a strong support for the healing you need during times of illness. "Bless the Lord, O my soul, and forget not all His benefits: who forgives all your iniquities, who heals all your diseases." (Ps. 103:2-3 NKJV)

RENEE'S EXPERIENCE

Sometimes it takes a time of suffering and physical weakness for a person to come to a deeper appreciation for the family and friends God has so blessed our lives with. We are all too familiar with the vow "for better or worse, in sickness and in health" yet it cannot perpetuate in our spirit until we have witnessed and experienced that vow being taken seriously.

My husband was a pillar of strength and light for me during a very dark time. We had certainly had our battles, our ups and downs, our stubborn mountains to climb, but I always believed that he was the man God had placed in my life and gave me a life partner. I have seen marriages and families crumble under the pressure of physical oppression. I have heard many who cannot bear to see their spouse suffering, and some who are simply too selfish to lay down their own lives at a time when their helpmate is desperate for help.

Brain surgery allowed me to see my husband in a new light. Yes, I knew he was a good man, but there were, as in so many relationships, my agitations and judgments I had harbored over only six years of marriage. I would never, in my wildest dreams, imagined that the day of "sickness and in health" would knock at the door of our marriage so early on in our walk together. Actions that I would have perhaps expected to ensue in old age (bathing, dressing, serving as a walking crutch, driving, doing the laundry, caring for our 4-year-old daughter so mommy could rest) suddenly became stark realities. My husband had the patience and grace to complete every task that emerged after a craniotomy, from the expected to the unexpected.

Emotionally, I was an utter wreck for months following both surgeries. We "brainies" experience many side effects for months to years after brain surgery, that leave even the most equipped brain surgeons perplexed. Every day I would wake up with a different challenge, a different symptom. Aside from the Lord himself, my husband was my emotional support on these difficult days. When brain fog and dizziness loomed before me, he was the one praying over me, holding my hand, and declaring my healing by the blood of Jesus. "I would have lost heart, unless I had believed that I would see the goodness of the Lord In the land of the living." (Ps. 27:13 NKJV)

This scripture resonates in my spirit when I think of how the Lord blessed me with a husband who would stand by me during a time when I had truthfully "lost heart." The Lord's goodness shines through to give us a living hope in Christ, and he uses his very children to elicit this type of love. My husband was fulfilling his role as my helpmate. As Christ loves the church, his bride, Rolando took his vow with all seriousness and humility. Sure, we laughed when he had to wash my hair and help me get dressed. I would not trade these moments for painless ones because I know that the Lord was strengthening our marriage through my weakness and vulnerability.

Your trial, the disease that looms over your life, is not given to you by God, but the Lord can use it for His end-all purpose to heal, restore, or strengthen the relationships that already exist in your life. In the days following my diagnosis, I would often pray Jesus' prayer from the Garden of Gethsemane: "... and fell on His face, and prayed, saying, "O My Father, if it is possible, let this cup pass from Me; nevertheless, not as I will, but as You will." (Matt. 26:39 NKJV)

Yet, deep down within our soul, there is a longing and hope that if we suffer, there will be a time of peace, prosperity and newness to follow. Undoubtedly, my husband and I have experienced a new season in our marriage as a result of my near-death experience, and I wouldn't trade that for any cup. Do we want to endure the trial? At the time, no. But I would not trade the harvest of joy that follows the storm for any instantaneous healing.

The effect of sickness affects different family members in different ways. My four-year-old daughter did not have the capacity to truly understand what was going on, but her spirit sensed it and was truly affected. I will never forget the fear that bleakly swept over her the day they positioned the "nodes" all over my head and face (including areas of my hair they had to shave) in order to navigate my brain during surgery. This was done several days before the actual operation, and my daughter literally curled up in fear and pain when she saw me. Even at her age, she suddenly understood that mommy was going through something. Even after I assured her that I was fine, and the doctors needed to play a video game on my head, she did not believe my lie. For months after the surgery, she suffered from anxiety attacks at home and in pre-school. We were grateful that her teacher was so understanding of the situation and she was a strong support and Christian example in my daughter's life during my recovery. Perhaps the most difficult challenge for me was dealing with feelings of self-consciousness and judgment from other parents when my daughter had her attacks. I knew exactly what it was she was dealing with, but others who did not know the full story were often perplexed and judgmental. This allowed me to grow as a mother and as a Christian. It made me realize that we should never judge each other based on our children's behavior. We can never fully understand or know what goes on in the lives of others that can affect our children's behavior. It also opened the door for the Lord to move in my daughter's life. She is no longer affected by anxiety, and she even received the award of "faith" at her school that year. In fact, to this day, she continues to remind me that I am "healed." When I get into a "complaining" mode about the hearing loss in my left ear, she is the first person to remind me that Jesus is my Healer: "Mommy, don't say that anymore. God is going to heal you!" she firmly reminded me just the other day.

I also thank the Lord for all of my family who were so supportive during my time of recovery. My mother, my father and his wife, and other friends in Christ dropped everything to come and be with me, and even take me into their homes as I healed. Even though there were some insensitive reactions I received from people or "friends" (and sadly this is also part of the journey) I am irrevocably grateful for all of the love and support I was and continue to be blessed with. We were never meant to live this life alone, and truly the "body of Christ" plays such a significant role as we each embark on our personal journeys of healing.

ENCOURAGEMENT FOR YOU

We want to challenge you, to take some time in prayer, to draw close to the Lord and ask Him to show you who He has put in your life as your "rock" during this crazy and unforeseen season. We were not meant to walk this journey alone. Though you might feel alone, God will place people in your walk who will sustain you and draw you closer to Him. Pray fervently that through the pain and brokenness of physical ailment, God will heal and revive the relationships in your life that could be dying, unbeknownst to you.

"Most assuredly, I say to you, unless a grain of wheat falls into the ground and dies, it remains alone; but if it dies, it produces much grain." (John 12:24 NKJV)

Jesus was speaking to his disciples of his coming suffering and sacrifice, and of the harvest that would ensure because of his faithfulness in the trial. Something has to die for life to grow, for the blessing to multiply. If we can truly die to our disease through the process of waiting for the fulfillment of the healing, then not only will we be blessed, but the relationships in our life can even experience a revival. When Jesus died on the cross, his suffering paved the way for a worldwide resurrection. Imagine how your suffering can open a door for the people close to you to not only serve you and sustain you in a time of need, but for God to rekindle and bring new life to the relationships with those closest to you. It could be your father, mother, children, siblings, friends and church family. When we endure a time of suffering, God will reveal to us the people who will truly "mourn with those who mourn, and weep with those who weep." It is a desperately glorious time to build, restore, and find joy in the relationships that God has so blessed us with.

CHAPTER SEVEN:
A HEART OF
THANKFULNESS

Thankfulness is a critical component of our healing process. A heart void of gratitude can delay our complete state of healing. Scripture shows us time and again how pertinent our thanksgiving is to the move of God.

Let's take a look at the ten lepers that Jesus healed on his way to Jerusalem. The men first cried out to Jesus and had faith to follow his instructions. In our trials, do we first cry out to Jesus and follow His instructions? When Jesus died on the cross, healing was ours, we have access to it and we can receive it because it belongs to us. We have all been given this measure of grace. But we shouldn't want to stop there; we should want to be made whole because there is a difference between healing and (wholeness = soul; mind, will, emotional healing). All of the ten lepers were healed, but only one became whole. That one came back to offer thanksgiving to Jesus from a heart that really understood the source of the healing. This leper recognized that "Every good gift and every perfect gift is from above..." (James 1:17a)

You see, the lepers had to go to the priest to be declared healed, but it was expected they would acknowledge God. They were healed but only one was made whole. Healing can come in various ways and healing is sometimes a process. We thank the Lord for our healing, but it is in our continued relationship and commitment to God that we are made whole. So many times, people forget that it is God that orchestrates everything.

He may use multiple pathways to make it happen, but ultimately, it is the Lord that deserves praise for it. Jesus told the thankful leper his faith made him well; a deeper level of healing, his heart was good and healthy and that's the reason he came back to give thanks. He had a deeper understanding of the sovereignty of Jesus. The thanksgiving wasn't superficial; it was deep-rooted in his heart and his thankfulness was the fruit of his faith. Our hearts have to be full of the understanding that we cannot, have not, and will not be able to do anything without God. We all need healing in some area of our lives, it may not be a physical healing, but there may be a time when you are hurt emotionally and will need the Lord to heal that pain. We have to recognize our need for God beyond the pain we currently have. We have to draw close to God in all things because this need for Him is what cultivates thankfulness and being made whole.

We have a responsibility in our healing. First to believe that Jesus has already died on the cross for our healing. It is His blood that has set us free from all sicknesses and disease. The other responsibilities we have in our healing are to walk in it, trust God and believe that it is already done, rest in His word and promises to us, and follow His instructions. Just like the man who Jesus told to go wash in the pool and be made whole. Jesus didn't heal him right away, the man had to do something to complete the healing.

LASHANDRIA'S EXPERIENCE

I always thought I was naturally thankful, until I became ill. It's downright easy to be thankful when things are going well, when we are being blessed, when we have a loving family, a roof over our heads, and a job we enjoy. It can be easy to fall into the kind of mindset that says, "I am unworthy, but God has still blessed me, and I am grateful." It sounds like a humble-enough statement, doesn't it? Yet, I have never experienced and struggled with real, deep gratitude until the trial of health complications arrived. God does not give us sickness (this is a result of the curse in the beginning of creation- we explain this in previous chapters) but he can allow us to journey through such weakness to cultivate a pure and holy "attitude of gratitude." This type of attitude does not come easily, nor does it come without a price.

There is a price that is paid when you are facing a chronic illness, affliction or death. In the midst of it, the first response is definitely not to thank the Lord for all that you are going through. In fact, you begin to question and get angry and feel afraid, thankfulness is nowhere to be found in the picture. How can I be thankful when my body is severely cramping non-stop with pain as strong as labor contractions? Who would be thankful while that is going on?

Honestly, it is difficult to have a thankful heart in the middle of pain or to remain consistent in thanksgiving. All you want to do is cry, yell, scream, and make it all go away. It wasn't until after the second surgery, once my body had started to regulate, that I really could understand thankfulness in this whole journey. But that was just the tip of the iceberg when it came to understanding to "give thanks to God in all circumstances." It wasn't until active recovery when I saw that all I had been through was indeed good. It was good because God had turned it around and made it good. It was good because of the increase of my faith that I gained from drawing upon the word of God. It was good because it produced in me more of Jesus than I had before it. It was good because now God could work through me because in my weakness, He is made strong.

But he said to me, "My grace is sufficient for you, for my

power is made perfect in weakness." Therefore, I will boast all the more gladly about my weaknesses, so that Christ's power may rest on me. 10 That is why, for Christ's sake, I delight in weaknesses, in insults, in hardships, in persecutions, in difficulties. For when I am weak, then I am strong. (2 Cor. 12:9-11 NIV)

I cannot say that I fully have mastered an attitude of gratitude, but it was in the weakest place in my life that God revealed to me who He is and for that I am thankful. I am still learning thankfulness in everything, as there are dimensions to the wisdom of God. It is in knowing God, not just knowing about Him, that we can begin to understand giving thanks to Him in all things. Even when it didn't feel good or make sense, if nothing else all I could say was "Thank you Lord, you are in control." The price to pay is high, the sacrifice is great, and no one will ever know what you experience. This was a part of my cross to bear; it wasn't easy, and yet I am thankful. I will never forget what I have been through, but I choose to rise above it and use it to help others. It shapes me, causes me to grow, and adds depth to my purpose, but it doesn't define my identity. Yes, it is true dealing with a chronic disease is like hell. All kinds of emotions will come including sadness, frustration, and anger. Some days all you want to do is cry and other days you feel angry because of the situation you are in. Some days you may just feel numb to the experience. It's okay to feel what you feel but choose not to stay there. This is, of course, a process though. No one automatically experiences pain and thanks the Lord for it. This is a behavior and attitude that has to be practiced, developed, and realized through the understanding that Jesus will work it out for us. "In your anger do not sin: Do not let the sun go down while you are still angry." (Eph. 4:26 NIV)

Choose how you see yourself, either as a victim or a victor!

After the surgery and especially the recovery as I began to feel a little "normal" again, I knew that the surgery was the right choice and I was thankful for the surgeon, but ultimately I knew it was the Lord that healed me. I was so thankful to God that He guided me to make that choice. God will and can use whatever He chooses to get you what you need. God always gives the best and good gifts to His children and it is not His desire for us to be sick physically, mentally, emotionally, or spiritually. "Beloved, I pray that all may go well with you and that you may be in good health, as it goes well with your soul." (3 John 2 ESV)

For me, my responsibility was to take some natural steps in improving my eating habits, my stress levels, increasing my spirit man, and allowing God to show me how to live in my body, mind, and spirit the way He intended for me from the beginning. For example, if you know that you shouldn't eat a certain food because it could hinder your healing, then that is an instruction that should be followed. This is the essence of faith because faith requires action. Belief requires action; it's not just a mental concept. If we are to believe and receive our healing, we have to take action and do our part and allow God to do His part. Faith doesn't make life and trials easy, but it does make it possible to endure and overcome.

With healing and being made whole, we have to take this posture and attitude: God you step in and I step back and when I do, God you can work it out. Ultimately, I have to let go. Honestly, this letting go, especially when your body is in pain and your mind is in a battle, is not easy to do. With everything feeling out of control, it may feel like you want to keep an ounce of it, but I assure you the best place to let go is in the hands of the Lord. Many times I would question why? What did I do wrong? But my question should have been, and with time has become, what are you trying to teach and show me through this? What am I gaining from this? Sometimes you may never know why it happens, but can you be okay with not knowing? God really can hold it all together if you let Him and teach you even through the pain.

RENEE'S EXPERIENCE

"In everything give thanks; for this is the will of God in Christ Jesus for you." (1 Thess. 5:18 NKJV) The Bible talks about giving thanks in all circumstances, and how often we quote this scripture in church, but how many of us can truly be thankful at the brink of death. It can be a bittersweet struggle to say "thank you" when you are in agonizing physical pain, and you know that death might be around the corner. The following scripture might even be a reality check (and secret thought) for many of us struggling with this kind of sacrificial thankfulness. "For in death there is no remembrance of You; In the grave who will give You thanks?" (Ps. 6:5 NKJV)

If we are truly honest with ourselves, this scripture is more aligned with our thought process at moments of hopelessness. It's kind of like, "Hello, God. Are you there? You see, I know it might be my time to leave this world, but how can I be thankful when I'm gone? So, um, maybe if you just give me a few more years, then I will be forever grateful."

It may sound immature, childlike, but this place of vulnerability and truthfulness can bring us to a deeper place of gratitude in the tough times. Sometimes it takes a near-death experience to fully realize (mentally, emotionally, and spiritually) that God has rescued us both from physical death, and ultimately, from damnation. At times of uncertainty, we can know one truth, and that is that we have eternal life through Jesus Christ. That truth, alone, is enough to be forever grateful for.

I will never forget the night I was diagnosed in the ER. The doctor was wise in how he presented my diagnosis. "You do have a large brain tumor, BUT it is benign. "I remember crying tears of joy and thankfulness when I heard this, as well as my husband. And we did thank the Lord in prayer that bleak day. However, not knowing the battle that lay ahead of me, as I look back, I am not sure I would have so willingly said "Thank you" if I had known how difficult a journey this reality would pose.

Yet, God wants us to give Him thanks, regardless of our emotions and regardless of how desperate we may feel. Over the course of a year and a half, I am still learning what a holy life of gratitude is. I wake up one morning feeling healed, whole, physically capable of conquering the world, and it's quite easy to say a heartfelt "thank you" prayer. Other days I wake up with brain fog, dizziness, feeling like I'm walking on a moving boat, ringing and utter deafness in one ear, and the horrible thought that maybe God didn't actually heal me. These times are the most challenging, yet the most important to verbally express what I am grateful for. The enemy wants to steal the song in our heart; his desire is to see us lose a heart of gratitude. That is why it is so important to verbally thank the Lord, each day, for what he has brought us through. And we must thank Him even on the days when we don't "feel" thankful because true gratitude in the Spirit is not an emotion, it is a truth.

After a time of depression following my surgery, I realized that part of my frustration was rooted in my inability to thank the Lord on the harder days. It was so easy to praise Him when I made it out of surgery and deadly complications thereafter, alive, but oh how quickly I forget about all He had mercifully saved me from since that time. Once I came to a place where I could verbally, in prayer, express my gratitude to God, thanksgiving became a natural reaction. Sometimes the simplest prayers and conversations with the Lord are the most powerful and carry the greatest healing power. Once you start your own list of thankful prayers, you will find it hard to stop thanking him. The list is virtually endless.

In the declaration of praise and gratitude, we are speaking prophetically to our situation, no matter how hopeful it looks through the eyes of our flesh. Begin to profess your thanksgiving with the belief that God has done it, and he will do it again!

Thank you that I am alive, another day.

Thank you that by your mercy and blood I AM healed.

Thank you that no weapon formed against me will prosper.

Thank you for satisfying me with long life and showing me your salvation.

Thank you for restoring to me my health.

Thank you for making me more than a conqueror.

Thank you that you shall bring none of these diseases upon my family or myself.

Thank you that I am your child.

Thank you....

Declare your healing and profess your thanksgiving through faith. By practicing a heart of joy and thankfulness, you will begin to reap the fruits of the Spirit, especially love and joy. I remember often feeling that perhaps God did not love me as I thought He did (a blatant lie from the enemy) or that He was punishing me by giving me a brain tumor (also a lie from the father of lies). But through practicing a spirit of gratitude, we become more aware of God's vast and unconditional love for us, as well as our true identity in Him

Dear sister, I hope and pray that you can come to a complete, unwavering understanding and knowledge of the perfect love of God. God understands what we go through.

For we do not have a high priest who is unable to empathize with our weaknesses, but we have one who has been tempted in every way, just as we are—yet he did not sin. Let us then approach God's throne of grace with confidence, so that we may receive mercy and find grace to help us in our time of need. (Heb. 4:15-16 NIV)

Jesus empathized with every single person He healed in the scriptures, and it is no different for you. Did he not weep when Lazarus was pronounced dead? Did he not have compassion on the woman with the issue of blood? He loves you so, and it is purpose and desire for you to be healed and made whole. Enter into His presence to thank Him for this unconditional love and experience the unlimited power and presence of His Holy Spirit. Our gratitude opens doors to our hearts that allows for His healing and grace to enter in and take control.

ENCOURAGEMENT FOR YOU

We encourage you to recognize God as your healer, thank Him for it, and draw even closer to Him each day as you walk in an awareness of His grace. What action steps can you take as you exercise your belief that you are healed? A heart that is cultivated for thankfulness sometimes has to experience difficult things. We go through trials so God can show up and show us and others that He is real. May your prayer to God be "Show me how to live." Show me how to trust you, and how to depend on you through this affliction and throughout my life. Help me to see myself healed. Help me to believe and experience your perfect love and grace through this process. Thank you, Jesus, for loving me, healing me, and saving me."

CHAPTER EIGHT:
A GLIMPSE OF GOD

There is nothing like facing the threat of physical death in one's life that will cultivate a sudden and eye-opening realization of eternity. When we are young, healthy, and untainted by the enemy's attacks over our progress, it is easy to lose sight, or never completely see, into the eternal realm. Sometimes God allows our physical senses to be tampered with so that our spiritual senses become more sensitive to His sense of time, as well as his eternal kingdom.

RENEE'S STORY

"Kingdom Seeking"

Maybe you have experienced a similar awakening in your own life as a result of physical pain and illness. I remember one of the first "attacks" against my health, and the sudden realization of the brevity of our days here on earth. Thoughts loomed in my mind as I attempted to comprehend how I could possibly face the threat of dying from a growing brain tumor, an illness beyond my control, so early in life. I was only 35, and I still had dreams and ambitions that were not fulfilled. My husband and I had been trying for a second child (our daughter was already four years old), we were searching for our first home (we had lived in an apartment for three years), we were developing a ministry as semi-newlyweds, and I was hoping to re-establish the teaching career I had begun in Arizona in my new home in San Antonio, Texas. It was a daily battle in my mind to accept that I was not immune to the diseases of the fall. I would cry out to God, fervently begging for healing, sometimes only giving Him the reason that, well, I was just too young to die.

I now look back at those moments as opportunities for a deeper revelation of His kingdom, and my purpose in His kingdom. After going through the initial pain and shock, the Holy Spirit helped me to change my "woe is me" thoughts into prayers for God to use me in His kingdom, no matter how few days I might have left on this side of heaven. He changed my perspective into a "let's work for the kingdom" attitude. I can't deny that the temptation is still there to shift my thoughts to self-pity and doubt, but I have discovered that when I start my day with a kingdom approach, my life becomes more focused on eternity rather than self-pity and moping.

When Paul endured persecution for the sake of the Gospel, it only heightened the ministry God had given Him. Because of his jail time, threats of death, and thorns in his flesh, Paul was accelerated in the ministerial purpose God had instituted in his life. It was when Paul was able to conquer the fear of suffering and death that he was able to overcome the confinement of the fallen world, to thus shift into the everlasting and vast possibility of the eternal world, Christ's Kingdom. In today's church we often speak of a "Kingdom perspective," and this is vitally important to the role and purpose of Christians as we prepare ourselves and others to spend eternity in heaven. However, it is not until we experience a true taste of eternity that we can understand and enter into our roles within His kingdom, now.

If you have ever been on the brink of physical death, you have been granted an incredible blessing and "sneak-peek" into the celestial and everlasting plans God has for His people. We must learn to recognize these moments as God-given windows to see into God's future plans for His children. God can allow our circumstances to light a fire within us that will jumpstart our work for His kingdom and likewise, diminish the plans that the enemy had when illness was brought upon us. This is one incredible way that we can fight the devourer. "The devil has come to steal, kill, and destroy. I come that you might have life and have it abundantly." (John 10:10 NKJV)

What is abundant like in the midst of physical pain and suffering? It is clinging to, trusting in, and believing that eternity waits for us on the other side. It might not be your time to be with Jesus, but He can use the "close call" to awaken in you and rekindle your love for Him and for His work.

I felt like I was serving the Lord before I fell ill. I was teaching overtime at both a public school and private ballet academy. I was serving with my husband in the ministry, as well as directing a dance ministry at my local church. I realized through my time of suffering, surgery, and healing (and this is still a daily process) that God was not calling me to "develop" the ministries He had given me, He was calling me to walk in blind obedience. God began to place people I didn't even know in my life (divine connections) to speak words of encouragement, to lift up, to share the Word, and to lead me into a better understanding of the body of Christ.

A month post brain surgery I joined a Facebook group for acoustic neuroma survivors, in hope that I would find comfort in hearing from others who were recovering from and still living with this type of tumor. I found my heart hurting for these people because many of them did not know the God who had saved them from death; many were bitter, angry, and fearful of what the future held for them. I started spending time responding to their posts, trying to share the Word and offer encouragement, especially if they were on the brink of the surgery. I met one woman who was convinced she had an acoustic neuroma and was posting questions relentlessly on the page. When I answered her and shared a verse of encouragement, she responded right away and asked to be my friend. I prayed with her through the week that led up to her MRI, and when she found out that she did not have a brain tumor, but a much more manageable and less life-threatening neurological condition, we rejoiced together. Despite the scare she had, her faith had been rekindled, and she had learned to seek the Lord again in a time of uncertainty and fear.

I am still learning how God can use me and my experience for His kingdom. I have found that putting a "title" to this ministry, or even trying to place my own selfish parameters on the work is of no value. When God wants to use you and your affliction for His glory, obedience and daily submission is of essence. When I came out alive, I wanted to start a healing ministry, a place where people would gather to be prayed over and divinely healed. Although this could very well still be part of God's plan, I have found that God desires my submitted heart to his daily assignments, rather than a man-made edifice or idea for ministry. God will share His glory with no other, and that includes my own personal ideas and opinions that are often very self-centered. He has placed person after person in my life to pray for, to encourage, to share His word, and to sow seeds with the hope that my experience can even foster a sneak-peek into eternity for others in the brethren.

My friend, you may feel terribly alone in your experience. You may battle with the fear of death every waking minute. But God is his infinite power and grace and wants to use your experience to kindle a fire of Kingdom knowledge and awareness in others. Will you be a conduit for the kingdom, or will you remain trapped in doubt, hopelessness, and physical limitation? We serve an eternal God, in whom there is no beginning and no end. When we seem to have reached our end, it is only the beginning. God wants to use you in the short number of days you have on his fallen earth. Will you embrace the mentality of His Kingdom, that others too may catch a glimpse of the streets of gold that await you and I?

"He who has an ear, let him hear what the Spirit says to the churches. To him who overcomes I will give to eat from the tree of life, which is in the midst of the Paradise of God." (Rev. 2:7 NKJV)

LASHANDRIA'S EXPERIENCE

"The Love of God"

"See what great love the Father has lavished on us, that we should be called children of God! And that is what we are! The reason the world does not know us is that it did not know him." (1 John 3:1 NIV)

I came to understand deeply how much the Lord loves me. He doesn't love me because I do everything right, in fact I mess up so much, yet he still loves me. I discovered the depth of His love for me through one of the most trying times of my life. Going through a storm, through a valley, through pain. I found that Jesus cares about me and understands what I go through.

I also saw the kind of love God has for us one day when my daughter was running and jumping on the couch. She fell and bumped her leg and started crying because she was in pain. It was pain that was caused because of her actions of not listening to stop jumping and playing around. I knew that she needed me to hold, comfort, and tell her it was going to be okay and to try to ease the pain.

I thought about how this applies to God and us, how he

loves us unconditionally whether we make choices that lead to the pain we experience, or whether things just happen to us that we have no control over that causes pain. In either situation, God is always there, ready to pick us up, comfort us, and love us. God eases the pain regardless. He's a comforter and He wants us to comfort each other from that same comfort He offers to us. God cares when we hurt and are sad.

That's the kind of God that we serve, that's the kind of love that a mother gives to her child, and that's the kind of love that the father gives to us. He gives us the strength that we need to get through it and the grace that we need to walk through it. I experienced this throughout my journey. I didn't always recognize it, but it was there- the unconditional love of God.

Will you allow the Father to take you in His arms to love and comfort you? Will you allow Him to ease your heart and your pain? Even as you may be struggling with an affliction now, God's love covers you. "But you, Lord, are a compassionate and gracious God, slow to anger, abounding in love and faithfulness." (Ps. 86:15 NIV) "He heals the brokenhearted and binds up their wounds." (Ps. 147:3 NIV)

I could have easily been upset with her, and for a short moment when she first started crying, I was a little upset because she was told to stop jumping and she knew that was the reason why she ended up getting hurt. She didn't listen and follow directions and that was a consequence of her actions but I could tell that she really needed me to hold her, comfort her, and ease her pain and through the process of doing that all of my anger went away. I couldn't be angry with her because I want to just love her, hold her, and take the pain away.

Our God is our protector; He's a comforter who comforts us when we are weak and when we are in need of him, He's always there. There is something we have to realize about physical affliction; it is an attack from the enemy. It doesn't matter how it presents itself, if it is any kind of sickness, disease, or ailment it is from the enemy. Everything comes from either love or fear. But we know, as the Word says, that perfect love casts out all fear. So love triumphs over fear, therefore, translating to God triumphing over the enemy. God is love and the enemy is the father of lies, and fear is a lie. Everything God does is from a place of love. His heart towards us is love and as we walk through difficult seasons of life, our faith to help bring us through must also be rooted in love. The word says in Galatians 5:6 AMP, "For [if we are] in Christ Jesus neither circumcision nor uncircumcision means anything, but only faith activated and expressed and working through love."

So yes, faith without action is dead, and yes, it is impossible to please God without faith, but faith requires love. It works through love and we have to have love in our hearts and show that love to others. This is what God was showing me as I loved and comforted my daughter. This was what I experienced all around me as I was going through my journey of sickness and healing. I saw and felt not only the love of God but also love from others. If there was any negativity, my family did a great job of safeguarding me from it. All around me was love and I believe that is what created an atmosphere for my faith and the faith of my family to work. Our faith was able to grow and produce good fruit because of love. I also believe God, in His faithfulness and because of His love for me, orchestrated it that way and it was crucial to my healing.

Even now a few years after the illness and surgery, God is yet showing His love and faithfulness to me. I recently experienced something that could have been a setback. I was experiencing an attack and my intestine was beginning to shut down. I don't know if I had some type of infection trying to manifest or what, but nevertheless, it was an attack. My husband and I recognized it immediately and began to pray and declare the word of God over my body. We went into spiritual warfare and drew close to God calling upon His name and healing scriptures. I laid down and fell asleep and my husband continued praying. The power and manifestation of God's presence was heavy in our room and my husband said he saw Jesus come in. The Lord came in His love, faithfulness, and promise to me that I am healed and touched my body. In the morning, I woke up feeling much better with no symptoms of what I had experienced the night before. God healed me and stopped the attack on my body. Before, I probably would have gotten scared and allowed the attack to exacerbate, therefore resulting in a trip to the emergency room. But this time we exercised our faith and drew close to God and He showed His word to be true that by Jesus' stripes I am healed, and no weapon formed against me shall prosper. This kind of faith came from the trials we had already experienced and learning and growing in God's word. We went to God first and trusted Him, and honestly this is something that I have to continually learn and put into action. One thing I know for sure is God's love for us is real and when we tap into Him, He can show us personally how much He cares for us. "I love the LORD, for he heard my voice; he heard my cry for mercy. Because he turned his ear to me, I will call on him as long as I live." (Ps. 116:1-2 NIV)

Dear sister, let's draw close to the Lord and take a few minutes to praise Him for His faithfulness and love, to rest in His arms, and to seek Him wholeheartedly as He uses our testimony for His glory. Pray this prayer: Heavenly Father, thank you for loving me without limit. Even when I have forgotten you in times of trouble, you have never forgotten me. Thank you for eternally accepting me as your beloved daughter- healed, holy, and favored. Lord, let me know deep within my soul how much you love me, even when fear and doubt try to attack my mind. Jesus, help me to look beyond my hurt and pain to understand and follow the destiny you have designed for me within your kingdom. May your unconditional love and grace empower me to be a light to others as we live for your kingdom. In Jesus mighty name, amen.

CHAPTER NINE: AFFLICTION DOESN'T DEFINE YOU

In the book of John Chapter 9:1- 41 NKJV, we learn about a man born blind who miraculously receives His sight after Jesus commands His healing. I have always been perplexed at the question posed by His disciples when they ask "Rabbi, who sinned, this man or his parents, that he was born blind?" (John 9:2 NKJV) Jesus replies, "Neither this man nor his parents sinned, but that the works of God should be revealed in him." (John 9:3 NKJV) Upon executing the prophetic act of anointing the blind man's eyes with clay and saliva, the man is healed, and his sight is restored. What a marvelous miracle! The man begins rejoicing and claiming Jesus as God saying, "If this man were not from God, He could do nothing." (John 9:33 NKJV)

Ironically, the Pharisees enter into the picture to not only discredit Jesus' healing power, but to remind the once blind man that his testimony means nothing because he is a sinner deserving of his lifelong disability. The Bible even says that they then cast him out for being healed by Jesus. Sadly, this can happen to many of us that have lived through physical affliction. We receive the healing we have so desperately prayed for, yet others doubt that we have truly been healed by God's hand. They may question legitimate healing for various reasons. Maybe they are like the Pharisees, and they believe our sickness is some form of divine punishment. Or, perhaps, they are jealous of the move of God in our lives. There are others that simply lack the faith to believe that God can heal in such marvelous ways today. Whatever the opinion of others, we must fully accept and embrace our healing trusting that God wishes to glorify Himself through our overcoming. It is through this experience that we can begin to look beyond the illness, the difficult memories and painful past, to a future in which our testimony becomes of sewing ground to reveal the glorious works of Jesus.

Even if you are in the midst of a stormy battle with disease, you can believe that your experience will end with a powerful testimony that will magnify the Lord and bring hope to others. The blind man was not concerned about his past, even when the Pharisees attempted to diminish his testimony. He did not allow his disability to define Him, but instead chose to move forward and use his healing to proclaim and believe in the name of Jesus. Whether you are currently fighting illness, or you have been healed, God does not want the affliction to define you. Rather, his desire is to see you walk out of the fiery battle without the stench of fear and inadequacy but shining with a new light that reveals His power and purpose in your life.

LASHANDRIA'S EXPERIENCE

I used to look at my scars and think they were ugly. I was ashamed of my struggle and even though my body was healed, I still had to address the need for healing in my emotions and how I saw myself. I had to start healing the pain I felt about the way my body looked and the changes I experienced about the way I went to the restroom. I had to work on some soul healing, and over time, the more I drew closer to God and talked about what I was feeling with others, the more I could trust, and adjusted to my "new normal" I could start to see the scars as my testimony of how God brought me through.

The scars tell a story of how I overcame, and they help give me a reason to keep resting in the promises of God. My scars show my fight and how I won and stand today to share with others. The enemy came after me, but I overcame. My journey isn't over; it's just beginning. My latter will be greater. "'The latter glory of this house will be greater than the former,' says the LORD of hosts, 'and in this place I shall give [the ultimate] peace and prosperity,' declares the LORD of hosts." (Hag. 2:9 AMP)

I am stronger today than I was, but it has been and continues to be a journey and I never would have gotten to this point without God first, my family and friends, and my will to fight. Sometimes you have to learn to fight to live and fight to be healthy. Not fight in the physical sense but fight spiritually by putting on the whole armor of God and using the weapons God gives us even in times of hopelessness. The Word, our words, worship, praise, and faith (believing) are not clichés; they are powerful and real. You have to allow the Word of God to become your revelation and truth. Until the word becomes real and until Jesus becomes real to you, the manifestation will not come. The blood of Jesus broke all infirmities, that's where the healing is, in the blood. Plead the blood of Jesus over your body, over your mind, over whatever needs healing. See Jesus coming into the situation and see your deliverance. Jesus has to be bigger than the disease, illness, or trial. Jesus is bigger! "The thief comes only to steal and kill and destroy; I have come that they may have life and have it to the full." (John 10:10 NIV)

The enemy's job is to kill, steal, and destroy. He comes to stop us from having hope and faith in Jesus. He comes to stop us from realizing our power over him. He comes to steal our joy and cause us to quit and be stuck so we can't move and manifest what God has for us. The enemy comes to mess with our minds, our words, our will, and he wants to separate us from God and others. He wants to keep us from fulfilling our purpose and he wants to give us fear and doubt. The enemy wants us to be sick and he wants us to think that healing is not possible. The enemy is not our friend, he hates us and he will use whatever and whoever, including ourselves, to stop us.

But we have authority and power over the enemy and anything he may bring against us. We have more power than we know and think. That's why he tries to defeat us because he knows we are greater than him. God has given us authority over the devil. Be proactive even before you face a trial, speak the word of God over yourself and your family, declare yourself healed, see yourself living life abundantly, walk in faith, think in faith, live in faith. Build yourself up in faith so that if something comes that you must go through, you have the word in you ready to come out and stand on.

RENEE'S EXPERIENCE

For several years after brain surgery, radiation, and regular check-ups to ensure that the residual growth was not coming back, I lived in daily fear and anxiety. I have been tempted to allow one-sided deafness, nerve irregularity, facial spasms, and "wonky head" syndrome to define me, but I choose not to. Rather than dwell on the repercussions of a brain tumor, I must choose each day to walk victoriously, to not allow these lingering symptoms to define who I am. I believe the Lord can use my experience to bring hope to others, but I also pray that people who do not know my story yet, will be amazed when they hear it and witness the healing power of God in my life. When many others had to relearn everyday actions such as walking, talking, and swallowing, I was able to return to teaching soon after surgery. This is solely the grace of the Lord. Although it didn't come with ease, I had to make a choice from the beginning whether I was going to allow my disability to control my destiny, or my destiny to overpower my disability. God has equipped us for every good work, and his strength is sufficient because of our weakness. On days when I am tempted to wallow in or complain about some of my physical deficiencies, I am reminded of just how far the Lord has brought me, and I am thankful. I am thankful that sickness does not control me, and I am grateful that my identity is in Jesus Christ. My prayer is that, just like the blind man Jesus healed, my testimony will live to glorify Christ, not to glorify the affliction.

As painful and frightening as illness, and facing physical death can be, I have never experienced the love and faithfulness of God as powerfully as during this battle. I have come to believe that God is truly real and He is the epitome of love. These battles may challenge our faith in ways we have never imagined, but this is when the Lord comes in as our defender, as our healer, and as our destiny definer. "So shall they fear the name of the Lord from the west, and His glory from the rising of the sun; when the enemy comes in like a flood, the Spirit of the Lord will lift up a standard against him." (Is. 59:19 NKJV)

Through trial and suffering, we have the incredible gift of intimately comprehending the depth and strength of God's divine love. We also have the choice to fear or to believe. "For God has not given us a spirit of fear, but of power and of love and of a sound mind." (2 Tim. 1:7 NKJV)

When the enemy tempts us with thoughts of doubt and unbelief in God's healing power, and darkness creeps in, all we have to stand on is God's promise. Even after God has allowed us to conquer, fear is our greatest enemy. If we allow that fear to control us in the aftermath, we will never fully enter into the destiny the Lord has designed for us. "And we know that **all things work together** for good to those who love God, to those who are called according to *His* purpose."

(Rom. 8:28 NKJV)

We can trust in and embrace God's purpose in those foreboding moments, when we ask "what if…" Is it not what God desires, but to be the object of our affection, and the only true Comforter? Illness is not an infliction God has cursed us with, as many believe, but when the devil launches His attack, will God not find a way to use it for his glory? His Word says He will, and if we are to live the abundant life after the battle, we cannot allow ourselves to be chained to the past. I am an overcomer through the blood of Jesus, and so are you.

ENCOURAGEMENT FOR YOU

All victory belongs to Christ Jesus as in 1 Corinthians 15:57 NLT: "But thanks be to God! He gives us victory through our Lord Jesus Christ." The victory not only comes from the healing, but it comes in the aftermath. How do you see yourself? We love that we do not look like what we have been through. We love that our minds are not stuck in a "sick or victim" mentality. We of course do not forget what we have experienced because it has shaped who we have become, but it does not define our whole existence.

Sister, we encourage you to see that what has happened is not your identity. It has shaped who you are, but it is not you. Please don't get engulfed in the illness but use it to create something good and productive. Use what you went through as a message to others that God is not through with you yet. Be empowered to stand and be a light to those who may still be in darkness.

It is a significant part of our lives, but we do not wallow in it, we use it as a testimony of who the Lord is. We could have easily died multiple times, but the Lord preserved our lives, our health, and our strength for a purpose. A purpose that is still unfolding and however God wants to use this, we yield to Him. The victory came when Jesus died on the cross for you and me. We can continually have hope in Him and the power we have through Him to overcome.

"I have told you these things, so that in me you may have peace. In this world, you will have trouble. But take heart! I have overcome the world." (John 16:33 NIV)

She Overcame! is a declaration that we can speak over our lives. Life is about trials and blessings. Other tests will come. Even after the healing, there may be setbacks or symptoms that arise or even another trial you may face. Just as Jesus said in the Word, "we will have trouble in this world." (John 16:33) However, by using the power given to us through the Word, finding our true joy and peace in a relationship with God, and keeping the faith that God has done it before and He can do it again, will be what you and I can grab a hold of. We also can stand on the truth that we are not alone because God is always with us.

Being an overcomer is not just about defeating the obstacle, but it's also about not letting the obstacle stop you and cause you to give up and quit when it's still there. *She Overcame!* is a prophetic declaration that God can, will, and already did it for us, therefore, we can walk in our healing and wholeness in all areas of life, and you can too.

Psalm 91 (NIV)

Whoever dwells in the shelter of the Most High

will rest in the shadow of the Almighty.

I will say of the Lord, "He is my refuge and my fortress,

my God, in whom I trust."

Surely he will save you

from the fowler's snare

and from the deadly pestilence.

He will cover you with his feathers,

and under his wings you will find refuge;

his faithfulness will be your shield and rampart.

You will not fear the terror of night,

nor the arrow that flies by day,

nor the pestilence that stalks in the darkness,

nor the plague that destroys at midday.

A thousand may fall at your side,

ten thousand at your right hand,

but it will not come near you.

You will only observe with your eyes

and see the punishment of the wicked.

If you say, "The Lord is my refuge,"

and you make the Most High your dwelling,

no harm will overtake you,

no disaster will come near your tent.

For he will command his angels concerning you

to guard you in all your ways;

they will lift you up in their hands,

so that you will not strike your foot against a stone.

You will tread on the lion and the cobra;

you will trample the great lion and the serpent.

"Because he loves me," says the Lord, "I will rescue him;

I will protect him, for he acknowledges my name.

He will call on me, and I will answer him;

I will be with him in trouble,

I will deliver him and honor him.

With long life I will satisfy him

and show him my salvation."

PRAYER OF SALVATION

"For God so loved the world that he gave his one and only Son, that whoever believes in him shall not perish but have eternal life." (John 3:16 NIV)

God gave us his best gift, his one and only son Jesus. He gave us love and that love set us free. As long as you are still breathing here on this earth, there is an opportunity to live the life God intended for you. Salvation is a free gift from God. If you are ready to receive this precious free gift, pray this prayer:

Jesus, I believe that you are the Son of God, the savior of the world and that you shed your blood and died on the cross for my sins, and you rose from the dead three days later. I confess my sins and ask for your forgiveness. I am ready to trust you, Jesus. Please come into my heart and have your way in my life as my Lord and Savior. Jesus, take up residence in me, and begin living through me. Amen.

If you have prayed that prayer, you are now saved! Welcome to the family of God. Continue to seek and draw closer to the Lord by reading, listening to, and studying his word, prayer, connecting with a Bible-based church, and other like-minded believers. Enjoy your new life in Christ and know that you are not alone! "Therefore, if anyone is in Christ, the new creation has come: The old has gone, the new is here!" (2 Cor. 5:17 NIV)

ABOUT THE AUTHORS

LaShandria Redman, also known as Nette, is an anointed worshiper, visionary, and leader who balances ministry and family. LaShandria has a Master of Arts degree in Dance Education and was the founder and director of Divine Appointment Christian Dance School for six years, located in Tucson, Arizona. She now serves as a fitness and health educator, a local dance teaching artist/specialist, and music teacher. LaShandria is the co-founder of She Overcame, a ministry that empowers women to go beyond the limitations of afflictions and overcome through the power and message of Jesus Christ! She and her husband Covito, who serves in the military, are the parents of three beautiful children.

Renee Castillo has had a God-given passion for dancing since the age of three. She has a Master of Arts degree in Dance Education from California State University, Long Beach, and is the founder and director of DANZAR ministries. Renee resides in San Antonio, Texas with her husband, a reverend, their 7-year-old daughter, and one more child on the way. She currently works as a local dance educator and choreographer and enjoys teaching online ESL classes to students in China. Renee is the co-founder of She Overcame!

Find out more about LaShandria and Renee at

www.sheovercame.org

CPSIA information can be obtained
at www.ICGtesting.com
Printed in the USA
FSHW021455280121
78006FS

9 781647 733162